Contracting Out For Human Services

SUNY Series in Urban Public Policy
Mark Schneider and Richard Rich, Editors

Contracting Out for Human Services

*Economic, Political,
and Organizational Perspectives*

Ruth Hoogland DeHoog

State University of New York Press   ALBANY

Published by
State University of New York Press, Albany

©1984 State University of New York

All rights reserved

Printed in the United States of America

No part of this book may be used or reproduced in any manner whatsoever without written permission except in the case of brief quotations embodied in critical articles and reviews.

For information, address State University of New York Press, State University Plaza, Albany, N.Y., 12246

Library of Congress Cataloging in Publication Data
DeHoog, Ruth Hoogland.
 Contracting out for human services.

 (SUNY series in urban public policy)
 Includes bibliographical references.
  1. Municipal services—United States—Contracting out.
 2. Public contracts—United States. I. Title. II. Series
 HD4605.D43 1984   352.1′626′0973   83-24292
 ISBN 0-87395-893-4
 ISBN 0-87395-894-2 (pbk.)

Contents

Preface — viii

1

Advantages and Disadvantages of Contracting Out — 1

The Case for Contracting Out 4
Review of Empirical Literature on Contracting Out 7
Problems and Limitations of Contracting Out 12

2

Three Additional Perspectives on Contracting Out — 17

Analysis of the Procontracting Argument: Three Conditions 17
The Economics of Market Imperfections 22
The Politics of Cooptation 25
The Process of Organizational Decision Making 28

3

The Human Service Cases — 34

Goals of the Research 34
Case Selection and Methods of Study 36
*An Introduction to Title XX Contracting Out
  in Michigan Department of Social Services* 37
CETA Contracting Out in the Michigan Department of Labor 46

vi CONTRACTING OUT FOR HUMAN SERVICES

4

Competition in Service Environments and Contracting Out Procedures 54

Competition in DSS' Service Environment 55
Competition in DSS' Contracting Out Procedures 59
Competition in the Employment and Training Environment 62
Competition in BET's Contracting Out Procedures 65

5

Making Contract Decisions 71

Why Contract Out for Title XX Services? 72
DSS Needs Assessments and Planning 74
Choosing DSS Contractors 76
Why Contract Out for CETA Services? 86
BET Needs Assessments and Planning 87
Choosing BET Contractors 88

6

The Watchdog Role 101

Review Procedures in DSS 102
Opinions about DSS Reviews 104
BET's Review Procedures 107
Opinions about BET Reviews 109

7

The Costs and Benefits of Contracting Out 113

The Costs and Quality of Purchased Social Services 114
Other Benefits of DSS Contracting Out 117
Perceived Problems of the Purchasing Process 119
The Costs and Quality of Purchased Employment Services 120
Benefits of BET Contracting Out 124
Perceived Problems of the BET Purchasing Process 126

8

Concluding Analysis of the Conditions
  and Perspectives on Contracting Out   129

Comparison of DSS and BET Contracting Out   130
The Realities of Contracting Out   133
The Three Alternative Perspectives   137

    Appendix A Methods of Study   144

    Appendix B Service Contract Interview Schedule   149

    Notes   164

    References   175

    Index   184

Preface

    This book addresses both the theoretical and practical aspects of one major form of public service privatization—contracting out for human services. My major aim was to consider this service delivery technique from various social science perspectives, since the realities of implementing social programs via outside agencies appeared at variance with the standard approach of public choice scholars who recommend it as a technique to cut costs and improve services. To determine if these alternative perspectives had any relevance to actual cases of contracting out, I examined one state's experience with purchasing services under two major pieces of social legislation of the 1970's. Thus, this is also a comparative work, in the sense that two Michigan departments and programs were studied and found to have interesting differences, as well as similarities, in organizational structure, contracting procedures, and service outcomes. The results of this exploration may prove disappointing to those who might expect a clear benefit-cost analysis or a practical list of do's and don'ts for improving service contracting. These were not the intent of this effort, though some may wish to extrapolate specific suggestions from the research. The reader who is curious, however, about the additional economic, political, and organizational perspectives and who is concerned about the human services contracting process will find something here of scholarly and practical interest.

    Since the time this book was first conceived and the research enterprise begun, a number of changes have occurred to alter the context of contracting out for human services. The Reagan administration entered office in 1981 with a new philosophy of federalism and the human services that promoted greater state responsibility and increased privatization of public services. Though it was an unanticipated development, this new emphasis on contracting out, among other privatization methods, gives additional relevancy to a study of human services contracting. The two pieces of legislation, Title XX and the Comprehensive Employment and Training Act (CETA), have been replaced by other programs; however, this examination of contracting under the two programs contributes to an understanding of contracting out in general, and may help scholars and policy analysts to evaluate attempts to use this service delivery approach more broadly.

I accumulated a number of obligations in the research, writings, and rewriting of this book. Many thanks are due Terry M. Moe, Stanford University, who, early on in my graduate studies, stimulated my interest in organizations and political groups, and became a constant source of advice, criticism, and support in this project. Gary J. Miller, Michigan State University, provided me with many helpful comments and unfailing encouragement. Jeffrey D. Straussman, Maxwell School, Syracuse University, first encouraged me to think critically about service contracting and to pursue an empirical study in the field of human services. His comments on a later version of this book were very useful. My colleague and friend, William Kelso, University of Florida, read various versions of the book and offered extensive and thoughtful suggestions for improvement. Others who read all or part of this book and provided comments were: Charles Press, Michigan State University; Jack Knott, Michigan State University; Mark Rushefsky, University of Florida; George Edwards, Texas A & M; Gary Wamsley, VPI; and anonymous reviewers. This book is much better for their criticisms and suggestions, but all responsibility for the final product is mine—especially since I failed to take all the advice I received.

I am also indebted to the many individuals who agreed to participate in the research for this book. Various officials in the Michigan Department of Management and Budget, the Department of Social Services (DSS), and the Department of Labor's Bureau of Employment and Training (BET) were very generous with their time and insights. In particular, Reginald Carter assisted me in getting interviews with DSS officials and contractors. Diane Emeling of DSS and Deborah Grether of BET were especially helpful in reading sections of the manuscript, providing additional materials, and giving useful comments on the details and process of contracting. In addition, the representatives of the contractor agencies were both friendly and helpful in giving me a broader picture of the service delivery system. I was impressed by both the officials' and contractors' professionalism and dedication.

Finally, I want to thank my husband, Bernie DeHoog, for getting me through this lengthy process of research and writing with special support and encouragement.

1

Advantages and Disadvantages of Contracting Out

The 1970s can be characterized as a decade of doubt, self-examination, and change at all levels of American government. Even though the sixties had produced many new ambitious programs, services, and bureaucracies, major problems were complicated by several other difficult issues in the seventies—the Vietnam War, Watergate, recession, energy shortages, inflation. The obvious inadequacy in dealing with these matters helped to produce a general distrust of government and government officials among many Americans.

This dissatisfaction with government has worked itself out in many ways throughout government. Proposals for tax limitations, spending limits, a federal balanced budget, and tax reductions have been particularly popular. Tax burdens have been perceived as being too heavy, considering that the quality of basic state and local services have not noticeably improved, and, according to many, some services have deteriorated in quality. Many ordinary citizens have not directly benefited from the social programs that have helped to increase their tax bills. As a result, they have offered increased resistance to providing generously for the poor and near-poor.

Although almost all areas and levels of government have been the object of criticism, the government bureaucracies have probably received the loudest, largest, and most vociferous criticism. This disapproval has taken at least two major forms. First, citizens have expressed a fear of the growing government bureaucracy interfering in and controlling many aspects of life. In particular, the private business sector has grown weary of trying to comply with government regulations being produced by bureaucrats. Second, dissatisfaction with the public bureaucracies' implementation of programs and their provisions of services has been rapidly increasing since the late sixties. Frequent have been the reports of wasteful and inefficient federal programs, deteriorating urban services, and ineffective attempts at solving problems and meeting needs. One is often left with the impression that there is little that government can do quickly, efficiently, and effectively.

What has been the response to these criticisms of government and the public bureaucracy? Recognizing the validity of many of the charges, elected and appointed leaders at various levels in government have tried a host of different ways to deal with these issues. They have attempted many policy and programmatic changes, and they have instituted or expanded a number of innovations to alter the way in which government operates; including budgetary reforms, and overall increase in rigorous policy analysis and program evaluation, the passage of federal civil service reforms, requirements for long-range planning, and several changes in the organizational arrangements through which services are produced, delivered, and consumed.

In particular, a preference for using nongovernmental agents has recently become a significant part of government theory and practice. Although for some years federal and state agencies have followed directives from the Office of Management and Budget and state administrations to rely on the private sector to supply their needs, only during the Reagan administration have we seen such a major commitment to achieving public goals and providing services via private agents[1]. In the field of human services, private, nonprofit agencies are expected to increase their services to the needy under the Economic Recovery Program. Urban enterprise zones are to be created to give businesses the incentives necessary to revitalize economically depressed areas. In its Government Capacity Sharing Program, the Department of Housing and Urban Development (HUD) has encouraged local governments to increase their use of contractors for a wide range of municipal services. A variety of mechanisms for privatization of public services has been suggested in the literature of public administration as well, including using vouchers, contracting out, load-shedding, coproduction of services, etc. Several recent books have proclaimed the advantages of these alternatives with such titles as *Better Government at Half the Price*[2], *Privatizing the Public Sector: How to Shrink Government*[3], and *Cutting Back City Hall*[4]. Most of these service delivery approaches have been considered or adopted by governments at all levels to cut back expenditures in view of fiscal constraints and to "get government off our backs." Perhaps the theme for the eighties will be less is best.

While all of these innovations warrant further examination, the process of governmental contracting out for the production and delivery of public services will be analyzed in detail in this book. The general term contracting out refers to the practice of having public services (those which any given government unit has decided to provide for its citizens) supplied either by other governmental jurisdictions or by private (profit or nonprofit) organizations instead of delivering the service through a government unit's own personnel.[5]

Given the historical and political framework provided above, we can consider contracting out as part of the effort of many governmental units to respond to critics, improve their performance, and cut costs. Contracting out for services from either the private sector or outside public agencies is not, however, a new method of service delivery. For years, many local governments especially have purchased such routine services as garbage collection, road maintenance, and street lighting from outside suppliers.[6] Under the contract cities plan (or Lakewood Plan), several California cities for some years have contracted out for their basic municipal services—in most cases, from the county government.[7] And almost all government units that require roads, buildings, or military weapons have long had contracts with profit-making firms for architectural and engineering services. On the federal level in the post World War II era, the number of contracts for scientific research, complex technical or evaluative services, and defense-related services increased rapidly.[8] Bruce L. R. Smith, a foremost scholar on federal contracting has stated that such extensive usage of private institutions is a central feature of any modern government.[9]

Nonetheless, what the sixties and seventies spawned was, first, a greater consideration of this practice as an alternative to traditional public bureaucracies for a *wide variety of municipal programs and services*, particularly in the face of fiscal strain;[10] and second, a much greater utilitization of contracting for new *social programs* for disadvantaged clients at all levels of government, often because of federal laws and regulations.[11]

The Case for Contracting Out

What then are the arguments in favor of contracting for public services? Why would this method of delivering services be considered by some to be superior to traditional methods? In the academic literature, one school of thought has provided much of the theoretical basis for this approach—public choice theorists who have used the language and methods of economics to examine public bureaucracies and public service delivery. Although there are several differences in subject, methods, and emphasis, the major underlying arguments of scholars identified with this group are similar.[12] These arguments and their proponents have been influential in convincing politicians, public administrators, and laymen to embrace attempts at privatizing government.[13]

Unlike other public choice theorists, this group has concentrated on analyzing the nature of goods and services and altering the structures by which they are supplied, with less concern for the voting and demand mechanisms or the patterns of metropolitan organization. Using a neoclassical economic framework, these public choice scholars argue that the competitive marketplace produces goods and services efficiently, whereas monopolies, whether public or private, tend toward both inefficiency and unresponsiveness. Since in most program and service areas, government agencies are service monopolies, the personnel are likely to behave in ways that promote their own interests at the expense of the interests of efficiency and the consumer/citizen. William A. Niskanen, among others, has argued that public bureaucracies are inefficient and expensive burdens because bureaucrats use their monopoly of information vis-à-vis the legislature to maximize their bureaus' budgets—a goal that, if achieved, is most likely to increase their personal rewards. Consequently, bureaus tend to produce too much output, exceeding the point at which benefits equal costs, thus leading to larger budgets, the inefficient use of public funds, and bigger government.[14]

The basic perspective of Niskanen and other public choice theorists who study the supply side of public services is to encourage governments to explore alternative methods of service delivery and to use quasi-market mechanisms for services usually produced by federal, state, or local government bureaucracies. For the production of mainly private goods (those that are highly divisible and packageable) that the public sector has traditionally provided, governments could try to return both the financing and production of such services to the private sector entirely (e.g., garbage collection). Or governments could provide vouchers to the consumers, thus subsidizing the consumer rather than the supplier of a service and thereby giving the consumer/citizen the opportunity for choice among various agents (e.g., education).[15]

One of the most popular privatization modes is purchasing public services from either other government units or private companies by means of a contract. In delineating the nature of goods and the efficient role of government, public choice scholars assume that few theoretical differences exist between public and private sector goods and services in how they can be *supplied*. On the demand side, governments act on behalf of consumer/citizens and use taxation and coercive authority to prevent free riders. Contracting out can be used for many services with either private or public good characteristics, according to E. S. Savas, since both types of goods need not be delivered to the public *by* a public agency *through* its public employees, even if the service is paid for by the taxpayers through a government unit.[16] Instead of using its own bureaucracy, the relevant government body can purchase the services directly from public or private sources through a process of competitive bidding or competitive negotiation, thus developing quasi-market conditions and achieving a desirable degree of flexibility and responsiveness.

The essential role of the government agency or elected body would be to perform a watchdog function. Not only would it deal with revenue gathering or budget allocations and the transfer of payments to the delivery agent, but the government unit would also choose the agents, continue to monitor and evaluate their performance, and engage in long-range planning. The threat of the government agency contracting with another supplier (or even producing the service itself) would, proponents believe, ensure that the producer is both efficient and responsive to the needs of the consumer/citizens and their representatives. Therefore, contracting out is expected to enable governments to achieve the best service performance at the lowest cost because of a direct monetary incentive — the profit motive and/or the desire to stay in business.

In summary, what then are the major arguments in favor of using outside sources to supply government services? First, proponents believe that private supply will lead to *lower government costs* for at least five reasons:

1. Competition for contracts would help to reveal the true costs of production and eliminate waste, since contracts would be awarded to those offering the most or best quality services at the least cost level.
2. Substitution of the profit motive for budget maximization and empire-building would help to limit budget growth in particular, and government growth, in general, in the long run.
3. Economies of scale could be realized in some jurisdictions through the reduction of overhead, start-up costs, or high personnel costs by spreading supply over a large number of units or other agencies (e.g., contracting for specialized medical services).
4. High personnel costs would be reduced, primarily due to avoiding public employee unions and public personnel controls (e.g., civil service rules).
5. Greater flexibility in the use of personnel and equipment would be achieved for short-term projects, part-time work, specialized needs, or new problems — without a commitment to sustaining a bloated bureaucracy.

This anticipation of reduced costs of public services is the most compelling reason for both scholars and government officials to favor contracting out.

A second advantage of contracting out is seen as an outcome of competition — i.e., it is expected that competition for contracts among private contractors will also produce better quality services for the price paid, since a direct monetary incentive for good performance by suppliers exists.[17] If the service delivered is judged to be inadequate by the overseeing agency, another supplier could be granted the contract (either another private agent or a government agency). To use Albert O. Hirschman's terms, the contract relationship has a major advantage over the usual methods; it allows for both exit and voice mechanisms to be activated in the event that the service quality declines or does not meet the contract's specifications.[18]

A third factor that some observers believe is a major advantage to purchasing services is that the rapid government growth of the last decades could be slowed, if not halted, by this means.[19] Government would have greater control over its services. The anticipated cost of savings would keep budget growth to a minimum, while the size of public employee rolls could be limited. The power of the centralized bureaucracy at all levels could be somewhat reduced as well, by allowing greater participation for private actors in public policy making. Public choice economist James M. Buchanan argues:

> *Governmental financing of goods and services must be divorced from direct governmental provision or production of these goods and services.* There may be fully legitimate arguments for governmental financing but little or no argument for governmental provision. Through the simple device of introducing private provision under government financing, the growth of public spending may, figuratively speaking, be stopped in its tracks.[20]

Review of Empirical Literature on Contracting Out

The obvious question that flows from the previous discussion is: Are these claims about contracting out verified by empirical research? The answer is—maybe. Most of the empirical works about contracting out fall into two categories: 1) studies of the *frequency* of contracting out in local governments and 2) studies comparing *costs* of services between in-house supply and contracted services, or public versus private provision of service. The first set of studies indicates that although a variety of services can be and are contracted out, the use of contracting out (at least at the time of the studies) is not yet widespread among local governments—only a few services are commonly purchased (e.g., solid waste collection, professional or housekeeping services).[21]

The second type of research generally focuses on cost comparisons, with some methodological refinements and additions in recent years. In part, the public choice confidence is based on these studies. In the main, what limited evidence there is usually supports the argument that the privately (or outside) supplied services are at least *less costly* (and in a few cases, more efficient) than in-house services, as in the cases of fire protection,[22] an airline,[23] a utility,[24] refuse collection,[25] a range of municipal services under the Lakewood Plan,[26] and property tax assessment.[27] However, these studies warrant further examination because they are commonly cited in the procontracting literature and, therefore, have influenced opinions and decisions about contracting out. This body of research has not provided clear-cut results, not only because of the narrow range of studies, but also because these studies are marked by several limitations and weaknesses.

First, some of the studies in the privatization literature are not about contracting out at all. Instead, they are primarily concerned with comparing *public production* with *private provision* of a service, in which the private agency, not a government unit, usually arranges the financing of the service through service charges to consumers (under a franchise or open competition).[28] Although suggesting that private supply is often less costly than public supply, these analyses do not specifically address the issue of contracting out, where private suppliers act as agents of the government through a service contract. A critical difference between contracting out and private provision is in the government's selection of contractors, its financing, and the oversight role. These factors change the process of service delivery and also may lead to varying outcomes.

Second, the privatization literature has done little to explain and distinguish the differences that exist between contracting out with private agents and with other governments. During the last two decades some scholars have examined the subject of purchasing a wide range of municipal services from other governments, as in Los Angeles County under the Lakewood Plan or contract cities plan.[29] Yet the more common instances of single service contracting between governments have hardly been researched by academicians.[30] Nor have we much insight about the relative advantages and disadvantages of public versus private contractors. What is needed is careful comparisons of the two forms in the several service areas where both types of contracting out are employed, with the goal of generating the conditions under which each type can be used to its best advantage.

A third problem with the empirical studies making cost comparisons is the difficulty in identifying and measuring all the costs associated with each service delivery alternative. Promarket analysts, such as Savas, have suggested that the advantages of private supply would be clearer if comparisons included equipment maintenance, capital expenditures, the full fringe benefit packages (including future pensions) of municipal workers, etc.—items that are not usually included in municipal service budgets by service areas.[31] James T. Bennett and Manuel H. Johnson argue that adding the opportunity costs of public production would also widen the cost differences in favor of private production.[32]

On the other hand, some of the costs connected with the contracting out alternative may also be underestimated. Critics of contracting out charge that government officials and researchers often do not examine the long-run costs of contracting out; simple before-after comparisons (though not generally used in the academic studies) understate actual costs, since new contractors will often bid low to get a contract, and then increase the amounts over time. According to some, various expenses associated with corruption in contractual dealings should be factored into analyses as well.[33]

Another type of cost that has been overlooked is the government's administrative costs of determining procedures and awarding, negotiating, writing, and monitoring contracts. These expenditures obviously are not reflected in contract amounts, but for some services (e.g., human services), they are probably substantial. In addition, municipal governments in particular are very vulnerable to contractor lawsuits contesting awards that increase the government's personnel costs. These many costs are difficult to measure accurately. They are usually distributed across various employees and units and may include the activities of both legislative and administrative officials.

Fourth, making interjurisdictional comparisons, a common method of research, can be a hazardous approach to studying contracting out or any other quasi-market mechanisms. Municipal and state budget systems vary widely from one government to another by including certain expenditures under different categories. Therefore, most direct comparisons are difficult to make, but without the full inclusion of the same types of costs, the results are questionable. The solution—to examine only units that have a mix of service delivery methods—reduces the generalizability of the research and limits the comparisons to only a few services where the mix is found.[34]

A fifth limitation of some empirical studies is that they do not go beyond the cost comparisons to include an analysis of the comparative *efficiency* of various arrangements. Municipalities have realized significant cost savings via contracting out, but the citizens do not necessarily continue to receive the same level or quality of service. If reducing service costs were the only goal of government officials, there would be little need to study efficiency. But usually decision makers want similar service delivery—or, on occasion, improved service delivery. The research of Savas and Bennett and Johnson indicates that private production or provision is often more efficient than public production in refuse collection.[35] However, David Lowery's study determined that though cost savings often are realized in contracting out for property assessments, the differences in service performance result in a less efficient service overall.[36] Like contracting costs, service levels and quality are frequently knotty concepts to define and measure, but the incorporation of both cost and performance elements will only yield more convincing results.

A further limitation of the contracting and privatization literature is that it includes studies of only a few public services. Some writers have generalized the mainly positive conclusions about these service alternatives to other public activities, including the human services.[37] Other scholars make an important distinction between purchasing hard and soft services.[38] While hard services may be purchased primarily to reduce expenditures, officials are less likely to be concerned with cost and more concerned with quality in the soft services, where the services are provided for clients. Not only may the procedures and outcomes of contracting out differ, but the methods of studying the two types are often dissimilar, and more problematic where human services are concerned. Service quality and effectiveness are the key issues, yet for each type of service, these elements are not simply defined and measured. Not surprisingly, few scholars have examined any of the large number of human, or soft, services that are purchased from outside suppliers.[39]

Related to this dearth of data in certain service areas is the lack of attention to the private, nonprofit sector that delivers many of the purchased human services. Generally the public choice and contracting literature has focused on for-profit firms that offer garbage collection, fire protection, tree trimming services, etc. However, some of the most interesting and complex contracting arrangements have developed with voluntary agencies of the so-called third sector. Donald F. Kettl calls this phenomenon at the local level part of the "fourth face of federalism"—where private agencies are instrumental in delivering services and meeting national policy goals.[40] To fully comprehend the differences and similarities between hard service contracting out with for-profit firms and soft service contracting with nonprofit agencies, we must have a better understanding of the incentives, structures, and operations of the voluntary sector.[41]

Finally, the field of public administration needs to examine contracting out more closely from another approach—that of understanding the contracting operation. With a few exceptions, the contracting literature has focused on the results of contracting out, not on the **process** of decision making.[42] The procedures of any administrative agency can have a positive or a negative affect on its services. Therefore, the actual regulations and behavior of contracting participants should be of interest to those who may wish to use this alternative to conventional bureaucratic supply. In this same vein, the political and organizational contexts of contracting out have been largely ignored in the empirical research.[43] Yet they offer fertile areas of study, simply because contracting decisions and results are not produced in a vacuum—they are the outcome of political and administrative pressures.

This brief review of the gaps in the present contracting literature is not meant to whet the scholarly appetite for a full treatment of all the issues and needs of the literature mentioned here. Rather, it is designed to remind the reader that many areas of government contracting out still require exploration; in fact, we know relatively little about the subject. These unexplored areas of research are critical to our improved understanding of the contracting process and its outcomes. If scholarly research in this field is to be of some utility to practitioners and elected officials in their decisions, we must begin to identify the conditions and procedures conducive to contracting arrangements achieving the aims of improved efficiency and good quality services.

Problems and Limitations of Contracting Out

Thus far, only the arguments favoring contracting for public services have been presented. But what might lead one to oppose changing the organizational arrangements for service delivery—changes which many believe will result in lower costs, good services, and a slowdown of government growth? Several different types of disadvantages and limitations of contracting out are recognized by various individuals and groups, including some who advocate the greater use of outside suppliers.

The first major problem with contracting for public services, raised by several different observers of public bureaucracies, can occur as a direct result of the relationships that develop between those granting the contracts and the private contractors.[44] Purchasing services from one or a few private suppliers on a continuing basis can produce cozy relationships that are highly beneficial for both sides, but may not be in the general interests of the taxpayers. In addition, conflict of interests and the use of bribes, kickbacks, and other illegal activities have been observed in many state and local governments and can be a part of any contracting system. As Lyle C. Fitch states:

> Contracts are one of the most common and lucrative sources of corruption in government. The abuse has been only diminished, not eliminated, by public bidding and other formalities designed to improve the integrity of the process. Private contractors doing business with the government are still one of the principal sources of campaign funds, and of support for shady politicians.[45]

In effect, the critics argue, corrupt or cozy relationships can help to erode both competition and quality control, which, in turn, lead to higher costs and lower quality services. Public officials will be more likely to make choices about public policy, service delivery, awards, and price based on the goals and needs of the suppliers rather than the needs of the recipients and the general public. Such kinds of criticisms, for example, have been leveled against the federal Department of Defense in its creation of a military-industrial complex based on contracting relationships. Most critics believe that the proper relationship between the government and its contractors depends on the government agency clearly being in control of the service and the private supplier. The government agency should set goals, draw up the proper procedures to encourage competition, and make careful performance evaluations in an objective manner.

A somewhat different criticism comes from those who are more concerned about private autonomy, particularly in nonprofit institutions. Their complaint about excessive government control is heard in regard not only to the general licensing, regulation, and limitation of the private sector but also to the contractual relationship.[46] Some fear that dependence on government contracts reduces the benefits gained from a thriving, self-supporting voluntary sector. Others wonder how church and state can remain separate when many church-related agencies deliver human services with government funds. Neil Gilbert summarizes how the problem of government control is viewed in the field of social services:

> A major concern from the perspective of voluntary agencies is the degree of autonomy they might have to forfeit in gaining access to public funds. The questions thay ask are, How much constraint on private agency activities will accompany the receipt of government funds, and will private agency activities emerge ultimately as merely the instrument of government policy?[47]

This concern does not call for the elimination of human services contracting, but it does emphasize that the granting of government contracts may produce difficulties in the short run and negative consequences in the long run for agencies that deliver public, as well as private, services. One of the real difficulties for government agencies arises in delineating clear but not excessively restrictive specifications, guidelines, and regulations for private agencies to follow in implementing public programs.

A third problem with purchasing public services is related to the two previous problems and is a major concern in any area of government. The ever-present political problem of accountability in public administration is only magnified with the addition of nongovernmental organizations carrying out the work of government. In a contracting system where structure (if it can be said to have one) is not hierarchical and where clear, straight lines of authority are often absent, political and legal responsibility or accountability to a chief executive or legislative body is said to be difficult to establish and enforce. Critics have charged that in almost any type of service it is usually more difficult for the public or program recipients to hold contractors responsible than elected officials and bureaucrats when the service proves to be unsatisfactory.[48] This problem is often complicated by the fact that nonprofit agencies can be torn in several different directions because of their need to be responsive to the various demands of the government, their boards of directors, their clients, and the community.[49]

A fourth difficulty with extensive contracting out can also arise, particularly in human services administration, according to some public policy analysts.[50] Because of a growing reliance on the use of private organizations, the creation and implementation of coherent public policy may become an even more formidable task for government agencies. This difficulty is particularly great in some service areas (e.g., day care, manpower programs, home health care) that utilize a variety of different private agencies with many of the institutions being concerned about maintaining their individual autonomy and accountability to other factors. Planning for and coordinating the multitude of fragmented activities of private service suppliers, according to this view, only adds to the already confused, overlapping, and complex divisions within our federal system of government.[51]

From quite a different perspective comes another argument against contracting out. Defenders of public employee unionization charge that this method of service delivery is a way of by-passing the municipal and state unions to use underpaid, nonunion labor. When governments decide to switch from public employees to private firms, union leaders accuse the offending agency of union-busting and putting public employees on welfare. A major obstruction to some municipalities in the Northeast and Midwest engaging more extensively in contracting out has been their politically powerful unions. In 1981, when the city manager of Benton Harbor, Michigan proposed laying off almost all public employees in the debt-ridden city government and replacing them with contractors, the most vociferous reaction came from the municipal union.[52] (Needless to say, the manager and his plan did not last very long once employees mobilized opposition to contracting out.) To support their interest in maintaining the traditional mode of service delivery, unionists are likely to employ some of the above criticisms in their arguments, often with the same type of ideological fervor that characterizes most procontracting works.[53]

Critics of privatization have responded to the argument that contracting out helps to limit government growth and interference, while at the same time strengthening the private sector and private organizations. They claim that the government's role in the economy, in private organizations, and in people's lives continues to grow but public employees may be hired less frequently to produce and deliver the public services. For example, in federal, state, and local governments, contracting out has often been used as a method of complying with imposed hiring freezes, while expanding programs and services that are increasingly expensive and intrusive. Along with a flourishing government role comes a growing tax burden for services and programs which governments believe they must provide. In her critique of using private institutions for public purposes, Brilliant concludes:

> Effectively, the mixing of public and private activities masks or screens the growth of government interference with the private sector and thereby makes it more palatable to average Americans. This illusion maintains the myth of less government, while government actually whittles away at the essential substance of private autonomy.[54]

Finally, some who recommend contracting out as a good alternative to bureaucratic supply have also pointed to some limitations of this method; it may not work equally well in all service areas. Niskanen, for example, states that in order to improve efficiency, payments to outside sources "should be in the form of per-unit output subsidies, and not lump-sum grants based on need or input costs."[55] This eliminates some public services whose outputs are difficult to measure accurately. In addition, Jeffrey D. Straussman has pointed out that the mindsets of elected officials and bureaucrats as well as various federal, state, and local laws may inhibit the adoption of contracting out.[56]

These are the major disadvantages and limitations associated with contracting out, according to a variety of analysts. This discussion does not imply, however, that contracting out for services is a uniformly undesirable alternative to bureaucratic supply. Rather, we are cautioned that the optimistic picture painted by contracting out advocates within the public choice tradition may have a darker side. A more balanced view can be gained by recognizing that the actual implementation of purchased services may not always conform to the ideal process model of contracting out and may also produce some negative consequences.

Conclusion

Many questions remain to be answered about implementing contracting out, several of them revolving around fundamental economic, political, and organizational issues. Some of these issues will be explored in the next chapter. The major question that needs to be addressed here and in the contracting literature generally is: How likely it is that contracting arrangements will achieve positive benefits in various services areas and under differing conditions? Can we say unequivocally, as a recent book proclaims, that contracting out produces better government at half the price?[57]

It is time that public administrationists go beyond the economists' deceptively simple cost comparisons of private versus public production of services to examine the contracting out *process*, including its political, administrative, and performance components. This effort may enable academicians and government officials to determine which services are suitable for contracting out, to identify and shape beneficial procedures, and to overcome potential problems. Chapters three through seven present an initial foray into these matters in the underresearched area of human services, specifically social services, and employment and training services. The results of the research indicate the complexity of the purchasing enterprise in these areas. Moreover, the process of human services contracting out sheds light on some questions that are of direct relevance to contracting out in general.

2

Three Additional Perspectives on Contracting Out

In the field of public administration, only the public choice perspective has offered a theoretical foundation for the favorable view of contracting out for services. The previous chapter's criticisms of this alternative have not been well-grounded in theoretical approaches to the general issues surrounding the subject, though they sometimes contain vague ideological overtones. However, there are other ways to look at contracting out—with the help of other, older intellectual traditions in the social sciences. Three different perspectives—one from the discipline of economics, another from political science, and a third from the multidisciplinary study of organization theory—offer useful frameworks for thinking systematically about contracting out. These perspectives suggest various disadvantages that could be associated with contracting out, and they point to underlying problems which would have to be overcome for its successful implementation. Before introducing and explaining these three perspectives, it is necessary to analyze the public choice argument to determine which conditions appear to be critical for contracting success.

Analysis of the Procontracting Argument

Various public choice theorists have focused on the positive expectations of contracting out. In particular, they argue that this innovation will lead to more efficiently provided services — lower costs (or increased output) can be realized. Additional benefits of this practice will include better quality services and a slowdown in governmental growth. For these expectations to be realized, however, some writers have implied in their descriptions of how contracting out works that certain necessary conditions must be present. To improve our understanding of the usefulness of contracting out, we must be able to begin to identify both the favorable and unfavorable circumstances and methods of contracting out. A more complete view of the process can probably enable decision makers to make better choices in service delivery issues.

Contracting out advocates maintain that the major benefits of contracting out arise out of the marketlike competition that is introduced into public service provision. When a government unit decides to purchase a service, monetary incentives are created for relevant outside suppliers to bid or submit proposals for the contract. Bidders/proposers must calculate not only the actual costs of service provision for the specified services, but also the price and services of other competing firms. According to the public choice (and market) theory, bidders will be encouraged to bid near the true costs of production for the exact set of services desired by the government in order to obtain the contract. To get a contract, in public procurement parlance, the bidder must also be viewed as *responsive* to the contract requirements and specifications as well as *responsible* — being capable of carrying through on the terms of the agreement. Given responsive and responsible bidders, contracting advocates assume that awards will usually be made to the lowest bidder, whether for garbage pickup, tree trimming, or employment services. Only then would there exist an incentive to keep costs to a minimum.

This simple model of the contracting process, however, depends upon the existence of certain key conditions, without which the benefits of using outside suppliers would not be fully realized. These conditions, though usually not clearly stated, are implied by the writers on contracting out, but they must be made explicit in order to understand the likelihood of attaining the expected benefits of contracting out. In particular, at least three major conditions appear to be critical to any contracting arrangements: 1) competition in the environment and in the government's contracting procedures;

2) government decision making to attain the goals of cost reduction and service quality; and 3) an effective watchdog role by government.[1]

First, public choice scholars emphasize that market competition is the key ingredient in reducing costs and improving service performance. Some writers seem to imply that the contracting market acts as an automatic mechanism, but this is a naïve view. In particular, two aspects of competition in the contracting system would appear to be essential—competition in the environment and in contracting procedures. The service environment determines the alternatives which can be considered by the government unit, as well as the calculations made by potential contractors. At least two responsible and responsive independent bidders or proposers (but preferably more) are required to produce a basis for competition. If no other firm exists to offer its services, what incentives does the single bidder have to pare costs and provide high quality services? And how can the purchasing unit evaluate the proposed price and services when there is no method of comparison? (This task is particularly problematic when the government agency has never delivered the service itself.)

In addition, the procedures utilized by the government unit must promote, rather than reduce, competition. Wide advertising, a clear and complete specification of the services required, and the impartial consideration of contractors throughout the process are the primary methods of ensuring that purchasing services will ultimately benefit the service consumers and taxpayers. Usually, maximum efficiency will be realized when the government has an adequate knowledge of: 1) potential service providers, and their past performance; 2) the services themselves, especially as they relate to the needs of consumers; 3) the methods of service; and 4) the costs of various components of the services. With this information, those who write the specifications and evaluate the suppliers' bids/proposals will understand what elements are essential, practicable, and sufficient for good service provision.

The second major condition for efficient contracting out that is assumed by contracting proponents is that contracting officials will be rational decision makers who are motivated for whatever reasons (reelection, altruism) to adhere to the goal of maximizing cost savings, with adequate service performance.[2] (This condition is hardly discussed in the contracting literature, partly, I surmise, because it is assumed that if contracting out is considered by officials, it is to achieve this goal of cost reduction.) First, individual public officials would be able to rank order the various alternatives according to this goal, with the information they have obtained about cost, quality, needs, past performance, etc. Then they would select the best choice—the alternative that will result in the desired services at the least cost level. This outcome, however, depends on two key elements: 1) the common goal of cost minimization with adequate service provision; and 2) sufficient information to consider the major alternatives and to judge accurately the anticipated performance and consequences of each alternative in terms of this goal.

This form of rational decision making should be used in at least three critical contracting decisions—the choice between in-house service supply and contracting out, the selection of services to purchase, and the choice among alternative outside delivery agents. It is probable that cost savings via contracting out can only be realized if it appears likely that outside sources would lead to reduced government costs (i.e., outside contractors should not be used simply because they are available or because politicians may benefit by it). And the service and contract award decisions must also be determined with this goal in mind.

The third general condition required by the contracting argument is an effective watchdog or oversight role by the government—a role which has been inadequately treated in the contracting literature. Unfortunately, the methods and techniques of program evaluation and contract management have seldom been applied to the subject of purchasing services in procontracting works.[3] The basic principle of contract administration is that the contracting officials should continuously monitor contractor compliance and service performance to ensure that the activities conform to the specifications of the contract. Where contractors are reimbursed for their costs, particular attention must be paid to verifying expenditures to prevent illegal activities and mismanagement of funds. Opportunities should also be provided for consumers of the services to express their suggestions and dissatisfactions directly to the responsible government unit. These monitoring operations are critical for spotting potential problems, keeping contractors honest, and providing technical assistance to contractors when problems arise. For human services (and any other types of services where cause and effect relationships are more uncertain), independent, objective evaluations are necessary to determine if the services are effective in meeting program objectives. These reviews of cost, performance, and effectiveness constitute essential feedback information when contracts are considered for renewals. Only by these means can the government be certain it is receiving the kinds of services it desires.

This analysis of the three major conditions—competition, rational decisions to achieve cost reduction and efficient services, and an effective government watchdog role—leads logically to this crucial question: How likely is it that these three conditions will be met in the real world of public bureaucracy? Since the positive expectations about contracting out appear to rest on these assumptions, what will occur if these conditions are not always present? These questions should be answered by thorough empirical study across a number of services in various government jurisdictions. Then better judgments could be made concerning when, how, and where to purchase which types of services. As yet, contracting scholars have not considered the importance of these conditions, nor have they examined them in their research.

Various social scientists suggest important ways in which the real world may conflict with the assumed, idealized world of public choice theorists. For our purpose, these social scientists can be placed into three groups on the basis of certain common themes in their arguments. I have labeled the three perspectives: the market imperfection perspective (from economics), the cooptation perspective (from political science), and the organizational decision making perspective (from multidisciplinary studies).[4] I do not intend to describe fully the analytic and historical bases of these perspectives. I will highlight their major arguments and identify some of their conclusions that can be extrapolated to the subject of contracting out. While they have different foci, arise out of quite different contexts, and do not specifically address the subject of contracting out, these perspectives suggest several ways in which the required conditions and, therefore, the associated benefits may not be found in some contracting arrangements.

The Economics of Market Imperfection

The works that might be considered part of this perspective on industrial organization are extremely diverse, but they are commonly rooted in a longstanding effort to move away from the idealized components of classical and neoclassical economics and to move toward a more suitable framework for describing and explaining the realities of economic behavior.[5] A major thrust of these scholars has been to emphasize imperfections in the traditional model of competition, pricing, information, and automatic adjustments of the market—market factors believed to produce an efficient allocation of society's resources. This neoclassical, competitive model underlies much of the public choice tradition's desire for market mechanisms in the supply of public services.

For this analysis, it is most relevant to examine two areas of supposed market imperfections—competition and information. According to this perspective, the market in many industries tends to be dominated by monopolies or oligopolies and cannot be described as competitive at all. Decision making within such markets is not characterized by a firm's automatic adjustments to the demands, prices, and competition of the marketplace; it is marked by market control or power, interdependence, and interaction in an attempt to reduce uncertainty and risk. Natural and erected barriers to entry into some markets, such as initially high capital investments, the absence of economies of scale, buyer monopsonies or oligopsonies, etc., significantly reduce the number of firms and the degree of competition. Consequently, prices are too high, output is too low, innovation and responsiveness to market changes are reduced, and resources are allocated inefficiently. Thus, traditional claims about the virtues of private sector activity and the unhindered marketplace may not always be valid.

The perspective of market imperfections also points out that buyers in the marketplace frequently have imperfect information with which to assess the products and services they wish to purchase. Not only is information limited and costly, but sellers have many incentives to distract, obfuscate, and mislead consumers with their prices, product varieties, packaging, advertising, etc. Since consumers, to a large extent, depend upon sellers' information, they may frequently make unwise decisions in the marketplace.

Some economists take this problem one step further. They point out that while perfect competition requires that demand and supply conditions be independent, in reality, producers influence demand. In this view, the classical belief that tastes for particular products and services are endogenous is naïve. The consumer seldom enters the marketplace with a self-defined idea of which products and services s/he requires. Instead, sellers often use selected information to mold consumer values and preferences, creating and shaping needs where none existed before.

Logical extensions of this perspective to contracting out lead us to question some of the major assumptions of the public choice proponents of contracting out, especially the competition and oversight conditions specified above. In many professional and technical fields and in services that require large initial investments for specialized equipment, there are often only one or two potential firms that could produce the desired service. The Department of Defense (DOD), for example, uses sole source purchase procedures regularly, often because only one contractor can produce the specified product or service. Competitive market pressures would certainly be minimal when the number of potential providers is so limited. There is no compelling reason to believe that outside suppliers will necessarily provide services more efficiently than bureaucratic agencies. Market power, monopolistic behavior, and the unavailablity of alternatives may easily translate into higher costs for taxpayers and lower quality services for consumers.

While in principle the government can replace unsatisfactory suppliers and contract with more efficient and effective ones or produce the service itself, this option will often be absent, because no other responsive and responsible contractors are available. When a municipality sells its own fire trucks, buses, or sanitation equipment in favor of contracting out, it greatly reduces the possibility that it can act as a potential competitor to private firms if their performance proved unsatisfactory. Sunk contracting costs and the need for service continuity may mean the government unit may have little choice but to utilize a particular supplier on a long-term basis. Therefore, the problem of service monopolies cannot simply be avoided by relying on the private sector, since the private sector itself may not be marked by competition among suppliers.

Part of the lack of competition in contracting out is due to the fact that government services often have some public good characteristics, as in fire protection, recreation services, education. The problem is not simply that this inhibits the expression of individual demand. Government can perform this function, though suppliers may try to shape the process. The more critical problem is that there is often no independent free market for supply purposes—the private sector is underdeveloped precisely because demand is underexpressed. When the government first articulates demand for a service, therefore, it has no full-fledged industry to turn to and cannot reap the benefits of competition through contracting out. Over time, its demand and preference for private supply can encourage the emergence of an industry which is, in effect, governmentally created and dependent. Supplier strikes, slowdowns, or bankruptcy are potential hazards to such government contracting. Reliance upon this kind of a public-private industry may produce far less efficiency and flexibility than the proponents of privatization expect.

Contracting out also requires a proposal evaluation and performance review process in which relevant, accurate, and complete information is essential for the government to judge costs, performance, and effectiveness, both before and during a contract's life. But the information the government requires for wise decisions is often difficult to obtain, for various reasons, including: objective information is so costly that only a limited amount can reasonably be purchased; service quality and program effectiveness are often difficult to define and measure; information is often collected through contractors themselves and other organizations that have many opportunities for screening, bias, and ineptitude; private contractors have incentives to shape information about needs and outputs to their own advantage. These sources of informational inadequacy suggest that the government may often make unwise contracting decisions.

The main point of this application of the market imperfection perspective is that the public choice model of contracting out is built on an idealized economic foundation. For various reasons, the conditions that are assumed to exist to produce efficient contracting out—especially market competition and adequate information—are not likely to materialize in the real world. Thus, the favorable expectations about contracting out will often be in jeopardy.

The Politics of Cooptation

While the perspective of market imperfections has dealt with economic matters, the cooptation perspective developed around political concerns. Some interesting parallels, however, between the two perspectives and their targets are apparent. Like the economists, political scientists who are part of this perspective reacted to the major paradigm of their discipline—pluralism. They did not accept the pluralists' idealized picture of competitive politics as a means of understanding the interest group system and its relationship with government.[6] A reasonable extension of this perspective to contracting conditions dovetails neatly with the economic perspective to produce salient caveats to the contracting model.[7]

In particular, these political scientists challenged the pluralist assumptions that 1) interests form spontaneously and naturally; 2) there is a natural balance of interests represented before the government; and 3) government acts as a neutral, mechanical referee of active interests in society. This cooptation perspective, especially as articulated by Theodore Lowi and Grant McConnell, emphasizes that different segments of government tend to be coopted, controlled, or changed by those interests which are most successful in organizing and articulating their interests.

For the cooptationists, some interests have inherent advantages over others in achieving organized political expression. Voluntary associations are more likely to form around the intense material interests of relatively few producers, these scholars claimed, than around the more diffuse interests of many consumers. In contrast to the well-organized interests of business, labor, agriculture, and the professions, a range of broader social interests (e.g., concerning consumers, women, the environment) have long struggled unsuccessfully to achieve membership levels and financial resources that reflect their support in society as a whole.

These biases are compounded, cooptationists argue, by the fact that the policy-making process is neither as competitive nor truly open as the pluralists assert. Because of their preponderance of valuable resources—votes, money, information, political support, administrative cooperation—the producer groups become the favored interests in their triangular relationships with certain key legislative committees and administrative agencies. Relationships in these subsystems often tend to be cooptative; each of the insiders gain through regularized, supportive relationships with other likeminded parts and through insulation from outside interference.

In the administrative process, cooptative politics is even more pervasive and deeply entrenched than in the legislature, as Lowi emphasizes. In order to survive and expand, bureaus try to mobilize political support through strong clientele relationships. Specialized interest groups often have so much to offer that they are formally incorporated into agency decision making, relied upon to perform governmental functions, and essentially, delegated public authority. Ties of professional backgrounds, friendships, and common interests mean that distinguishing between the government officials and the interest group or industry representatives is often difficult. Some analysts have pointed to the frequent career movements between the two sectors as a further indication of cooptation. Noticeably absent in all of this is input from those diffuse clientele, taxpayer, and social interests that have difficulty organizing and gathering resources.

From this perspective, contracting for services is likely to create more problems than it solves. To begin with, cooptationists would predict that potential or current contractors are far more active and organized than the recipients of public services, or those who pay for them—the taxpayers. The input from the private sector about service needs, methods of delivery, and the relative merits of private versus in-house provision would be heavily weighted in their favor. In the competition to land and retain government contracts, moreover, individual agencies and firms have every incentive to employ their resources strategically with bureaucrats and legislators to exclude competitors and gain privileged, regularized roles in the contracting system. They may also try to minimize any risks of competition by cooperating among themselves. With contracting out, in fact, the incentives for noncompetitive politics are even greater than they might otherwise be, because many of the suppliers become dependent upon government contracts for their very survival. Unless they find a special place in the contracting system, they are condemned to a year-by-year insecurity.

For their part, self-interested bureaucrats and legislators cannot help but see the opportunities for developing mutually beneficial relationships with contractors. Legislators have strong incentives to assist those contractors that have something special to offer, either directly (e.g., political support) or indirectly (e.g., economic advantage to a legislative district). Bureaucrats can give contractors special considerations in solicitations and awards and thereby achieve predictability, cooperation, and political support for their program areas. If desired, they can be afforded the future opportunities of private sector employment in the very firms or agencies they once awarded contracts.

This incentive structure generally means that, like the contractors, public officials will prefer to eliminate true competition in the contracting process. If they can, they will not design procedures that promote competition, objectivity, and fairness. Contracting decisions will not be characterized by officials seeking to lower costs, improve service performance, and slow down government growth. They have few incentives to make these their goals; they have many incentives to promote their own personal goals through contracting out.

For this and other reasons it is not surprising, as Smith notes, that federal contracts are "no longer predominantly set by competitive bidding as in an earlier and simpler day but are now to an increasing extent negotiated between the government and the contractor."[8] Senator Howard Metzenbaum (D.-Ohio) for some time has claimed that sole source procurement has become the standard because of friendships between Department of Defense officials and contractors, as well as loopholes in the federal procurement laws. In his opinion, these contracts have been the major cause of waste, inefficiency, and budget growth in the Department of Defense.[9] Other analysts argue that DOD weapons choices and other large contracts are also influenced by senators who desire the political rewards that come from representing the interests of major producers.[10] At the local level, city officials may confer contracts on hometown firms rather than outsider firms for political reasons.

The cooptative environment in which contracts are awarded also conditions the review process. Officials have few incentives to scrutinize compliance and expenditures or to conduct meaningful evaluations of service performance and program effectiveness. These types of information are not used for most contracting decisions anyway, since government actors often may not choose suppliers primarily on the basis of these factors. For other reasons, inefficient suppliers can be preferred to more efficient and effective alternative suppliers. Any incentive the government has to collect and employ evaluative data has less to do with truly objective evaluation than with constructing justifications for decisions that are made on political grounds. Thus, government oversight does not check cooptative politics. It simply contributes to the broader cooptative pattern.

All of this suggests that contracting out can be a counterproductive response to government inefficiency and growth. Contracting authorities are not interested in promoting the goals of contracting advocates—at least not in practice in their own bastions of power. Nor are they concerned with designing and implementing competitive procedures or thorough review methods. They *are* interested in maintaining existing relationships of mutual advantage and promoting new ones. These narrow interests are facilitated by more money, more programs, and resistance to any changes in funding levels, service priorities, and contracting methods.

Interestingly, this emphasis on the consequences of politicians' and bureaucrats' self-interest is not unlike that developed by various public choice scholars who favor contracting out as a method of getting away from the inefficiencies of bureaucracy. Gordon Tullock and William Niskanen, among others, posit that bureaucrats in particular are motivated to behave in their own interests, but these writers fail to recognize that these motivations may not automatically change when contracting out is introduced.[11] Contracting advocates generally dismiss the fact that officials may see opportunities in using outside rather than in-house supply.[12] Unless contracting systems incorporate new incentives to promote competition and maximize efficiency, why should we assume that contracting officials will change their behavior when purchasing services?

The Process of Organizational Decision Making

While the first perspective of market imperfections analyzes markets, industries, and consumers, and the second perspective of cooptation deals with the political relationships between producer groups and government officials, the third perspective focuses on organizations and organizational decision making. This last way of examining the subject of contracting out employs various concepts and conclusions from studies of organizations in the disciplines of sociology, psychology, economics, business, political science, and public administration.[13]

Paralleling the revisionist attempts of the market imperfection approach and the cooptationist school, decision-making theorists also reacted to unrealistic, conventional approaches to their subject—in this case, to the study of individual and organizational choice. Before Herbert Simon's work, most economists employed a concept of rational decision making in which individuals and organizations select the best alternative, following a thorough review and ranking of goals, alternatives, outcomes, and probabilities. Simon introduced a modification of this picture of "economic man" with his "administrative man," one who is "boundedly" rational. Because of limits on time, information, and cognitive abilities, individuals cannot be expected to consider all alternatives and their consequences each time a problem presents itself. Instead, decision makers primarily must rely on routine solutions (regulations, standard operating procedures) that reduce uncertainty, risk, and capriciousness. If an appropriate routine does not exist, one engages in a limited, sequential search process marked by "satisficing" behavior. According to Simon, individuals do not *maximize* goal achievement by examining many alternatives and rank ordering them, but they are compelled by their limitations to choose the first satisfactory solution.

In this perspective, organizational decision making is determined by one's premises or goals, information content and flow, the standard repertoires, and the threshhold levels of what is judged satisfactory. Political or organizational leaders do not provide the only means to control choices and behavior. Since decisions are determined by one's goals and information, personal (as well as organizational) goals, informal group pressures, and professional backgrounds are critical factors in shaping the premises of decisions. Richard M. Cyert and James G. March add that organizations often have highly ambiguous, nonoperational goals that make success difficult to define. The more operational, or actual, goals arise out of internal organizational bargaining and learning, and, as a result, are several in number and often in conflict.

Charles E. Lindblom's work on muddling through in public

policy decisions points out that goal agreement and a rational policy-making process is particularly improbable when many different individuals, groups, and organizations participate in decisions. Instead of seeking optimal, comprehensive solutions, policy makers treat problems narrowly and choose alternatives which are most acceptable to all involved. As a consequence, organizational or policy change is usually a slow, incremental, and piecemeal process. Past goals, decisions, and budgets are the best predictors of the future.

Applied to contracting out, this brief summary of the decision-making model of organization theory suggests that contract decision making often may not be oriented towards optimizing efficiency because it takes place in an organizational setting. First, government units may choose to contract out for a service in response to artificial, organizational incentives and not because of inherent cost or service advantages. Agency ceilings on personnel numbers, government hiring freezes, and the need to commit agency funds by the fiscal year's end provide reasons for using outside service suppliers. Under such circumstances, the contracted services may not be significantly better or less costly than those provided by in-house staff. Probably quite the reverse would often be the case.

Second, under conditions of fiscal constraints particularly, officials will not have the resources to make strictly rational decisions about outside supply, awards, and oversight. Instead of considering all available alternatives with a thorough search for relevant information about costs and service, they will satisfice. Only a limited amount of information will be obtained. Decision makers will cease looking for alternative service suppliers when a minimally acceptable contractor presents a proposal or bid. Unless clearly written into the law, the procedures of contracting out will be designed to find a suitable agent, not to promote competition through costly, wide solicitations and time-consuming procedures. Often officials will not pursue a thorough search since they can easily use previous contractors. Generally officials will try to avoid new contractors, different directions, and increased competition wherever possible. Standardized procedures and rules-of-thumb will help to simplify decision making, reduce conflict, and achieve contracting predictability for everyone.

In the third place, organization theorists would predict that government officials in the contracting process may not be interested in single-mindedly pursuing the goal of efficiency, as contracting advocates expect. Even if legislators or agency heads may wish to promote more efficient contracting procedures, subordinates often will not comply. They may have other operational goals that take precedence over the stated organizational goal. These operational goals may be formed by individuals' personal needs, professional norms, group or organizational pressures. Whatever the goals, they will determine whether outside supply will be adopted, which contractors will be awarded contracts, and the oversight methods utilized to ensure adequate service delivery. An inadequate watchdog function may be produced by limited organizational resources, the reliance on past decisions, and other decisional premises (e.g., desire to avoid conflict with contractors). Securing information to change future contract language and choices may be deemed unnecessary. Contractor performance will be judged by simple, obvious measures that flow from the goals of the organizational unit, instead of by measures that may be more difficult to obtain but more accurately reflect program effectiveness.

If more than one organizational unit or government level is involved in contractor selection, contract administration, and oversight, the difficulties involved in purchasing decisions will multiply. Units' goals will conflict, communication will break down, professional and organizational clashes will recur—particularly where the units have differing priorities and vocabularies. Moreover, often contractor agencies will have their own bureaucracies through which proposals are written and services are delivered. Not only does this fact make for a more complex process, but it also means that lines of accountability and communication may be more problematic than in direct service delivery or where a single unit is in charge of contracting out. For example, contracting for refuse collection by a small city council produces problems of a far smaller magnitude than when large bureaucracies, elected officials, and more than one level of government are all involved in purchasing services from large outside agencies.

This discussion of decision making emphasizes that privatization proponents should be aware of the variety of organizational contexts in which contracting out takes place. Several organizational factors combine to suggest that the contracting approach to services is not an automatic mechanism for supplying services, but one that is affected by various goals, organizational routines, information flow, and organizational structures. Instead of avoiding the major problems of bureaucracy, contracting out takes place in and is an integral part of an organizational environment. Consequently, at least some of the problems and outcomes of contracting out will be similar to those encountered in traditional service supply.

Conclusion

Is contracting out a viable solution to the related problems of government inefficiency, ineffectiveness, and growth? Contracting supporters in the public choice tradition have generally answered this question in the affirmative. The three perspectives introduced in this chapter, however, lead to a different response. Taken together, the economics of market imperfection, the politics of cooptation, and the process of organizational decision making suggest that the various conditions assumed by contracting adherents are unlikely to exist in the real world. Consequently, the positive expectations of contracting out will not materialize either. In this view, contracting out could even exacerbate the problems of government.

At this point choosing between the two sides is difficult and may not be desirable. Each perspective may not be an accurate model of a complex reality, both within and outside contracting systems. Each has, nonetheless, something to contribute to the study of contracting out. Each offers a different way of looking at contracting out, based on the assumption of certain distinctive conditions and behaviors in the world. Where those conditions prevail, the corresponding perspective will be most accurate in predicting human behavior and government outcomes. To achieve the beneficial effects of contracting out, at least three conditions appear necessary: competition, both in the environment and in procedures; incentives for decision makers to value efficiency and effectiveness; and an effective review process for expenditures, performance, and outcomes. The three alternative perspectives suggest the negative consequences that result when these conditions are altered or absent.

What is most necessary at this point is empirical research—

research that examines not only the outcomes of contracting out, but also addresses the conditions and process of contracting. Of particular importance is research that 1) evaluates whether the three major conditions assumed by contracting proponents do occur in various service areas; 2) explores the factors associated with these key conditions; 3) examines the linkage between these conditions and the outcomes of contracting out; and 4) determines if other conditions exist which promote the efficiency goals of contracting out or compensate for failure in the conditions. In the rest of this book, I will examine these four areas of research in two human service areas, using the three alternative theoretical perspectives. These areas of research have not been analyzed in the contracting literature. Yet they promise to allow us to identify suitable and unsuitable contexts for utilizing contracting out, and perhaps in some cases, to transform the latter into the former.

3

The Human Service Cases

The previous chapter has shown how public service contracting out can be understood from alternative economic, political, and organizational perspectives, in addition to the public choice perspective. The main question of this book is: Do these perspectives and their expectations about contracting out have any relevance to the real world of service delivery? The intent of this study is not, however, to test the four perspectives for general accuracy of prediction. That is a far too ambitious endeavor at this stage of the literature. Instead, we will focus on two cases in the human services to evaluate which of the various conditions and expectations associated with these perspectives are fulfilled in existing contracting systems.

Goals of the Research

Although any number of research designs, methods, and cases could be employed, several major goals guided the selection of appropriate ways to examine the subject of contracting out and evaluate the four perspectives. First, I wish to broaden the study of contracting to include services that have not been examined in depth by other scholars. Refuse collection especially has been quite thoroughly studied, with a few other services receiving somewhat less coverage, as indicated in the first chapter. At this point there is a great need to expand into new areas to determine if contracting out produces benefits across a range of services. In particular, my attention has been drawn to the human services where contracting out is frequently used but infrequently studied.

The second goal of this work is to focus on a different level of government besides that of the city—a unit that has been the site of most empirical treatments. Other governments, including states and counties, provide many services to citizens through contracts. The human services in particular are often purchased in highly bureaucratic settings where intergovernmental relations are critical factors. As a result, more individuals, units, and levels of government are involved in the process, producing a complex and challenging subject of study. In addition, the four theoretical perspectives are likely to have more relevance in the human services.

My third goal is to focus on the relationship between public agencies and private contractors. Although many of the human services are purchased from other public agencies, my attention has been drawn to the nonprofit agencies that the Reagan administration has called upon to supply more of the public services society wants. This focus can address some of the issues concerning the advantages and disadvantages of contracting that both sides of the contractual agreement may encounter.

The fourth goal of this research, earlier alluded to, is to consider not only the financial costs of contracting out, but also other significant costs and benefits associated with the practice and its procedures. In actual public decision making, cost is only one of several criteria used by administrators and politicians to evaluate the utility of any given change. Some of the additional considerations are suggested by the perspectives and their expectations; others will emerge from the research enterprise.

Finally, and perhaps most importantly, I intend to examine the contracting *process* and its procedures. The process itself will shape the results. Therefore, it is imperative to determine if competitive procedures, a rational decision-making process, and an adequate watchdog role are present in the human services. All four perspectives make different claims about how contracting out will work. To evaluate their relevance, we must emphasize the critical importance the process has on contracting outcomes.

Case Selection and Methods of Study

Because of these goals, this study examines state programs in two major human service areas—the social services, under Title XX of the revised Social Security Act of 1975; and employment and training services, through Titles II and IV of the revised Comprehensive Employment and Training Act (CETA) of 1978. To make the research enterprise more manageable, I focused on the process of purchasing services in two departments responsible for the implementation of these federal programs in Michigan state government—the Department of Social Services (DSS) and the Department of Labor (DOL). While they were not selected to be strictly representative of human services, these cases may illustrate some common patterns of social and manpower service contracting, since the federal regulations require the states to operate in somewhat similar ways.[1] In addition, the two cases will help to illustrate how different organizational, service, and political environments can produce somewhat differing procedures and outcomes. These federally funded programs may not, however, yield the same processes and results as would more independent state and local service areas.

Michigan state government is an interesting, important, and timely place to study human service contracting: a wide range of services are provided, many by outside suppliers; the systems of contracting out are fairly sophisticated and complex; and many citizens throughout the state are affected by these programs. In recent years, the state government has been carefully scrutinizing what it does, how, and why—in response to both changing federal policy and its fiscal crisis. Michigan state government has been historically viewed as quite progressive, particularly in its willingness to consider innovations and new programs. It saw a rapid growth in state services during the 1970s, with much of this growth occurring in the human services. During the late seventies and early eighties, however, it was plunged into such a downturn due to the state's economic depression that it was forced to reconsider some of its earlier choices to provide generously for many different human needs. Michigan may not, therefore, be considered a typical state; it can be viewed as a good choice to study simply because it continues to be a large and important state. Some of the issues that the state had to face for several years became of paramount concern to other states also struggling with fiscal stress.

Three major types of research methods were employed in studying the selected programs in DSS and DOL: 1) preliminary, open-ended interviews with twenty officials in four state departments to obtain an overview of state contracting; 2) a study of pertinent government documents, including a legislative evaluation study of DSS Title XX contracting,[2] the current annual plans for Title XX[3] and the Governor's CETA grants;[4] and 3) a series of in depth, structured interviews with an additional nineteen contracting officials and twenty service contractors. In the last and most critical phase, the personal interview with the use of a standardized interview schedule was the most appropriate method of obtaining information about the actual contracting procedures (especially as they related to the three conditions of contracting out and the viewpoints of those most involved in the process. (See Appendices A and B for a more thorough explanation of the methods and interview schedules used.) This research project was conducted between the summer of 1979 and the winter of 1981.

For the most part, this study depends upon qualitative, rather than quantitative, types of data. Unfortunately, reliable cost and performance data were not available from department files and documents. The major problem in studying human service contracting out, as found by Jeffrey D. Straussman and John Farie as well,[5] is that the budgeting and programmatic systems of the departments do not distinguish between direct and purchased services; and few services are provided through both means. Therefore, comparisons between private and public production are almost impossible to make, at least with "hard data." The interview approach, however, produces a rich supply of opinions and information that not only meets the research requirements of the theoretical perspectives and three requisite conditions, but it also suggests hypotheses that could be tested elsewhere.

An Introduction to Title XX Contracting in Michigan Department of Social Services

Three different types of individuals were used as information and opinion sources for this study of DSS contracting out: state DSS officials, county contracting officials, and contractor representatives. First, at the state level, six DSS employees were interviewed by means of interview schedules—two in programmatic areas (Adult, Family, and Community Services) and four in contract management. A mix of supervisors and specialists was interviewed. A second category of respondents was made up of seven social services or contract coordinators in seven county Departments of Social Services—from three of the four most populous counties in the state, with the remainder from medium-sized counties. (Small counties rarely contracted for more than one service.)

These state and local officials were selected because most of the DSS contracts originated and where owned at the county level, but were reviewed, processed, and monitored by the central contract management staff in the state DSS. State program officials interpreted county contracts for programmatic elements, and provided technical assistance to the field staff when necessary. As a result of these selection procedures, in depth information was obtained on several counties' contracting procedures from the county officials, and a more general overview of all the counties' contracts came from the state DSS officials. Consequently, most of the conclusions from this study apply to Michigan's Title XX contracting in general—not only in the selected counties.

The third group of participants in the research consisted of ten private, nonprofit agency representatives. Of the ten, two contractors had current statewide contracts that were drawn up and managed by state program officials, while the rest of the providers dealt primarily with various county Departments of Social Services. Because two of those current county contractors had contracts with more than one county, they were also able to provide comparisons and generalizations about the different counties' procedures and relationships. In addition to current providers, I selected two former contractors who had failed to have county contracts renewed. The names and agencies of all contractor respondents were provided by state and county interviewees.

Backgrounds of Respondents

Generally, the backgrounds of the three major types of individuals interviewed offer few surprises. The public sector employees differed little from the private sector respondents. The DSS employees were more likely than agency personnel to report some graduate educations, yet their degrees were in similar fields—usually social work. This similarity in professional and educational backgrounds indicates that public and private contracting participants probably have similar goals, information, and vocabularies concerning social services—factors that can foster better working relationships.

Contracting relations can also be improved by a personal understanding of the roles of other participants in the contracting process. Some respondents in all three groups had held previous positions in either state, county, or private agencies. For example, some county services or contracts coordinators had worked for the state DSS before, and others had previously been employed in private social agencies. In fact, two of the contractor respondents had moved from public to private positions (and vice versa for a county representative) that were almost direct counterparts in social services purchasing. Some involved directly in the contracting process suggested they may have been chosen for their current positions in part because of their appreciation for other viewpoints, as well as their wider knowledge. Several respondents reported that they felt they had a broader, more complete, view of social services as a result of their experiences.

In addition to additional knowledge about contract decision making and sympathy for the views of other actors in the system, private agency heads who have worked in DSS would also have the advantage of access to information and officials. One agency director, for example, had been influential in setting up the DSS purchase-of-service system in the early seventies, and had worked directly under the current state department director. Her experience and contacts made her an excellent choice for the position she now holds. It is also highly unlikely that her agency would have to fear losing the DSS contract.

The cooptation perspective posits that frequent movement between the public and private sectors of regulatory agencies can be an indication of cooptative relationships, in which public officials can lose their objectivity and the importance of their watchdog role. Similar situations can occur in contractual relationships. Cooptative relationships in the DSS contracting system are also possible because of the common educational and professional backgrounds. Therefore, the contracting procedures and the checks on the process by other officials are particularly critical.

Agency Profiles

The ten private organizations included in the sample indicate the diversity of social services providers used by the DSS. The services supplied to DSS clients by these agencies include money management counseling, geriatric day care, family counseling, vocational and educational services for the severely handicapped, health services for migrants, and family counseling for abuse prevention. The providers are fairly specialized agencies with a limited clientele and range of services. The sizes of the agencies in terms of full-time workers vary widely, from a low of three employees to a high of 155, with a mean of forty-four. Although one family counseling agency was established in the nineteenth century, all the rest have been formed since 1960—and several of these were in response to newly available federal and state human services funds.

All except one of the providers depended a great deal on government contracts. (The single exception was a state association of counseling agencies that subcontracted for all of the DSS services in a unique, one shot contract.) Of these nine agencies, five received at least seventy-five percent of their revenues from government contracts during the 1980 fiscal year. The ten agencies' total numbers of current contracts with various parts of the federal, state, county, or city governments ranged from one to sixteen, with a mean of four. (This does not include additional grants that some received from various private organizations.) In addition, several of the ten agencies have had previous contracts under Title XX or other programs that were no longer in effect.

While each agency had at least one DSS contract either currently or in the last few years, two had more than one contract at the time of the interviews—one homemaker agency had two, while a money management agency had contracts with ten different counties. Six of the contractors have had their DSS contracts renewed for many years. Three of these were started at the state level, and then became the responsibility of the county DSS. (Two remained state contracts and one was dropped.) The contract amounts varied widely, from a low of $4000 for money management in one county to a high of almost $1,170,000 for resident alcohol rehabilitation services that are available for eligible clients throughout the state.

Of the ten agencies included in this sample, at least five would be severely affected by major cutbacks or the elimination of their DSS contracts. If they did not find an alternative source of funding—a difficult proposition in these financially difficult times—some agencies would have to close their doors. Although DSS had at times encouraged contractors to find additional sources of funds and to use the DSS contracts as seed money, one contractor said there was little incentive to become more diversified in funding sources. He noticed that original government sources tended to pull out when others became available, and only continued to pay for programs that relied almost exclusively on their money. So the agencies gained very little by finding new grants and contracts.

This reliance on one or two funding sources, such as DSS contracts, can work both to the advantage and disadvantage of public service provision. If agencies are particularly dependent on large DSS contracts, they may be more responsive to government suggestions for improvement, since the loss of a contract could be devastating. Both contracting officials and providers mentioned that this responsiveness to correction sometimes has improved contract compliance and performance. On the other hand, there was evidence that contractor dependence could hamstring DSS officials if agencies: 1) mobilized their political friends, allies, and clients to prevent any change in program direction, priorities, funding, or awards; and/or 2) showed that their programs would not be delivered to needy clients at all if DSS dropped a contract. In these cases, the relevant government unit may not have had any choice *but* to continue contracts. Consequently, DSS would be contracting for services that were determined, not by service priorities and performance, but by the very fact of contractor dependence.

DSS and Social Services Contracting History

DSS aid to the poor and near-poor may be placed into three categories: cash assistance (Aid to Families with Dependent Children, direct relief), in-kind payments for goods and services

(Medicaid, food stamps, subsidized housing), and social services. Of these, not including administrative overhead, social services usually made up less than ten percent of the total Michigan DSS expenditures. Of this amount, approximately fifty percent of the funds were allocated for purchased services from private suppliers. Despite the relatively small amounts of money involved, purchased social services have been a politically and programmatically important part of welfare efforts at all levels of government.

Since the late sixties, several of the approximately fifteen general services for children, families, and adults in eight programs have been purchased from outside agencies and individuals under either agreements or contracts. Under *agreements*, the client (service user) selects an approved or licensed provider and together they work out the details of service delivery. The provider is either paid by the client with funds supplied by DSS, or DSS directly reimburses the provider (e.g., day care, home chore services). This research will focus on the *contract* approach to purchasing services, in which the county or state DSS chooses the provider and draws up a specific document outlining its requirements—type of service, number of units to be delivered, bookkeeping system, etc. In some cases, the provider may in turn subcontract with another individual or agency for actual delivery of some or all of the services for program recipients. In both cases, the county caseworkers must refer the clients to the appropriate service providers (who have been granted a contract with DSS) or arrange for an agreement between the user and service agent.

Purchased services under Title XX were financed in two different ways: 1) *straight* purchase, in which DSS paid providers with federal and state funds; and 2) *donated* funds purchase, in which public or private donations were made to DSS for one of the services and were used as the match for the federal funds. Donated funds could come from other state and local public agencies, or nonprofit and proprietary private agencies. This method was more frequently employed for contracted services, and therefore, will be examined more closely.

Most of the social programs in DSS were funded and regulated through Title XX of the amended federal Social Security Act (P.L. 93-647), that went into effect in 1975.[7] Title XX basically replaced most of the earlier titles of the act (Titles IV-A and VI). It authorized funding under a matching formula of seventy-five percent federal and twenty-five percent state monies for social services programs to low-income families and individuals for the primary purpose of reducing dependency.

Title XX essentially was a compromise document, designed to reduce some of the problems with the previous titles. It retained a $2.5 billion ceiling that had been placed on federal matching funds in 1972, and included some other stricter requirements to prevent states from spending federal monies on activities outside general social service goals. At the same time, however, the law and Health, Education, and Welfare (HEW) regulations allowed the states to continue to determine the specific services within those guidelines, the types of providers (in-house or contracted), and the procedures used in making these choices. Although the title required greater citizen participation, an annual plan before the allocation of federal funds, and encouraged greater decentralization of administrative decision making within the states, it continued to allow much discretion in implementation. As Andrew W. Dobelstein states, "According to this legislation social services are just about whatever states say they are, and they are available to whomever states want to have them."[8] Attempts to limit state discretion drastically because of previous exploitation of certain provisions in the law had been overcome by strong opposition from state governments, national welfare organizations, the Congress, and private agency groups.[9]

Although DSS has been purchasing services from various sources for several decades, from 1969-1976 DSS contracting out increased dramatically. Certainly the expansion of the welfare case load and the state of the Michigan economy during the 1974-75 recession contributed to the growth, but probably more important was the availability of open-ended federal funds and an altered federal policy permitting frequent purchase of services (the 1967 Amendments to the Social Security Act). As long as money was put up by the states, the federal government had to match almost any type of service at the seventy-five percent level.[10] According to a report by the Michigan House Fiscal Agency, Michigan's expansion in social services was due in part to pressure primarily from Governor Millikin's office and the state legislature to increase rapidly the level of federal participation in social services—the quickest method being to purchase from existing private agencies. Due to the donated funds provision in the law, DSS saw purchase as a way of expanding needed services with minimal state expenditure.[11]

Private or public agencies that could arrange to donate to the state the requisite twenty-five percent match for federal funds in turn received contracts to perform particular services. In effect, DSS "allowed private and local public agencies to determine the use of millions of dollars in federal funds with almost no effort to control the disposition of those funds or to account for their impact on DSS clients."[12] This strategy of using local provider/donors was fairly typical of the state governments, according to Martha Derthick, and contributed to the skyrocketing cost of the federal grant before the $2.5 billion ceiling was imposed in 1972.[13]

In addition, those committed to increased funding for the poor embraced the concept of purchase eagerly, since they saw that not only would it mean more services but it would also create a broader, state and national constituency for welfare and social programs—largely made up of public and private service providers, who might otherwise not act as advocates of the poor (e.g., traditional middle class agencies like the Boy Scouts, YWCA, United Way). Once that constituency was formed and became dependent upon DSS programs, the flexibility envisioned by contracting proponents was decreased, rather than increased. This state and local coalition, combined with allies in strategic positions, ensured that the new Title XX would not threaten existing arrangements.

In fact, Title XX encouraged continued growth in the social services, according to an Urban Institute report:

> Although service expansion was not necessarily the primary intent of Title XX when it was introduced in 1975, it is clear that a number of its provisions encourage this effect. Title XX changes program eligibility requirements to allow a state to service persons whose incomes are as high as 115 percent of the state's median income. . . . As a consequence, the legislation initially enabled (some would argue, encouraged) states to expand the *population* eligible for services. Similarly, the authorizations which allow states flexibility to determine the scope and nature of the *services* to be provided under the social services umbrella extend another opportunity for program expansion. Further, because it mandates an *open planning process* with increased citizen participation, Title XX provides a special opportunity for interest groups to place pressure on

the state to utilize all of the federal funding available to them. Finally, rather than serving as a control on service expenditures in states below their ceiling, that ceiling has instead served as a benchmark or a desirable program level, in effect stimulating program expansion.[14]

When it approached its limit on receiving federal matching funds in 1976, Michigan DSS began to reconsider some of its loose contracting procedures. Instead of purchasing almost any new service with the twenty-five percent match donated, and continuing virtually all previous contracts routinely, DSS sought ways to determine client needs and to compare the merits of current programs. DSS was not immediately successful in agreeing upon and implementing needs assessments and improved, competitive purchase procedures. But it did make some changes in the system during 1979 and 1980, in part because of the new provisions of Title XX. From the rather centralized, state-controlled process of the early seventies, DSS moved to a more decentralized system in which the county departments received allocations for purchased services and became involved directly in determining local needs, selecting providers, finding donors, and reviewing the services purchased for county residents. The result was greater variety in the contracting procedures and arrangements, since the counties were given some flexibility in this area. Although not strongly supported by state-level contracting officials, the change was part of the national trend toward greater local discretion in various programs which, it was hoped, would lead to a better allocation of resources. Not all of the contracts, however, were given over to the counties. The state program offices retained almost one quarter of the contracts that, according to some, were more politically protected or served clients statewide.

From this brief history of social services in Michigan, it is clear that the Congress, HEW, the Governor, the state legislature, and DSS officials have had quite different goals in using outside providers than do public choice proponents of contracting out. Those involved with the Title XX policy process did *not* seek lower costs or a slowdown in government growth—and probably not even better quality services. Instead, they aimed to provide a wider range of services for the needy, to encourage states to use both private and public sectors to accomplish this, and, at least for state officials, to capture ever larger amounts of money for state residents with few strings attached.

When funds became very limited in fiscal years 1980 and 1981 because of decreasing revenues and increasing social needs, the state and county levels were forced to examine both direct and purchased services carefully. Since all the structured interviews in this study were conducted during the summer through the winter of 1980-81, this crisis provided an occasion to analyze not only the general subject of social service contracting in light of the theoretical perspectives and conditions. It also illuminates the issue of the role of contracting out in times of fiscal stress.

CETA Contracting in the Michigan Department of Labor

The contracting procedures in DOL offer a necessary contrast to those in DSS, even though important similarities exist. I chose to study two special state governor's grant programs, under Title II and IV of the revised federal Comprehensive Employment and Training Act of 1978 (CETA), which are implemented in Michigan's DOL in the Bureau of Employment and Training (BET). (Since these interviews, CETA has been phased out and partially replaced by the Job Training Partnership Act of 1982.) Although the programs in DSS and DOL are both federally funded with the purpose of reducing dependency upon government assistance, the organizational environments and department goals manifest some interesting differences. In addition, the procedures for the two titles' contracts differed in certain key respects. First, probably one of the most salient differences between the two departments is that BET's CETA contracts are all negotiated at the state, rather than county, level. Second, state officials placed a three-year limit on most contracts, since many were for demonstration purposes. And third, in BET, donations were not required for most contracts. Under the Title IV youth grants, however, contractors had to match some of the total amount in the second and third years of the contracts. While all of these CETA funds were allocated among the states by use of a formula not requiring a match, Michigan's BET decided to require an increasing match to encourage the continuation of successful projects with local funds and support.

The federal government has funded a large number of employment and training programs over the last two decades in response to the needs of the poor and unemployed. In 1973, the Comprehensive Employment and Training Act (CETA) was enacted to consolidate many of the previous categorical programs into a new block grant. CETA transferred the planning and operation of such programs from federal and nonprofit agencies to state and local governments. This decentralized, noncategorical approach allowed state governors and local officials greater discretion and coordination in providing a mix of services in response to the needs of people in their jurisdictions within federal guidelines.

In the 1978 reauthorization, CETA underwent certain changes in the eligibility requirements, the number of public service jobs, and the state program. Several restrictions were adopted primarily in response to the severe criticisms of CETA programs. The most significant alteration was the shift in emphasis from public sector employment to private sector training and jobs.

Although most of the CETA funds have always gone to local prime sponsors (single units of government or consortia of local units), two titles of the revised act channelled funds to the state government. The political reasons for the Governors' Grants, as they are called, are clear. In the sixties and early seventies, many governors resented the federal government bypassing the states to offer assistance to local governments and private organizations. With the National Governors' Conference's congressional lobbying efforts, the states received grants for CETA programs through which they could more readily affect employment policies and services.

Specifically, the two Governors' Grants provided for innovation, experimentation, coordination, and certain direct services. Title II, Section 202 (b)(c)(d) and (e), authorized the Special Grant to Governors to develop and operate programs that addressed issues that were usually beyond the scope of local prime sponsor programs. (This type of grant was also part of the earlier Title I, with a few differences.) Although most of the funds were used for contracts with state and local public and prime sponsor agencies, a variety of coordination and special services contracts were made with a few private organizations. The goals of the Title II state grant were to provide governors and their labor agencies with funds to assist and coordinate local prime sponsors, to conduct labor market studies, to set up demonstration projects for groups not adequately served by local units, and to provide information and coordination with unions and other CETA-related bodies.

The other contracts examined here are funded under CETA's Title IV, Section 433 (a)(2) — the Governors' Special State-Wide Youth Services, a new direct services program for states. This program was designed to add model or experimental youth projects developed under the state government. For both titles, state officials could choose services from a list of federally approved services, but Title II included certain mandated activities as well. In Michigan, both public and private agencies could be used for these grants, but only a few private organizations received contracts each year.

While the goals and expectations of the CETA legislation and regulations may not have been to reduce costs and government growth by contracting out, the programs were generally designed to meet the needs of the employable poor more effectively — whether by in-house services or via contractors. In a sense, then, one of the goals of contracting proponents can be said to be found within the CETA legislation. The Governors' Grants allowed states to take advantage of the expertise developed by public and private agencies, to provide special services for certain target groups, and to encourage innovation in employment services. By focusing on the development of demonstration or model projects under CETA, Michigan DOL committed itself to choosing programs whose plans and past performance held the potential of being most effective in assisting the unemployed.

Unlike the Michigan DSS and Title XX, the federal DOL apparently did not want merely to spend money or expand services to the needy; an improved allocation of resources (including political control) was the objective. CETA was created to overcome various inefficiencies in the previous patchwork of manpower programs that had produced overlapping services, contradictions, inconsistencies, a lack of coordination, and federal goals that were incompatible with state and local needs.[15] The reauthorized form of CETA in 1978 also intended to reduce the dependence upon public service employment — work that often did not have direct applications to the private sector. While not specifically aimed at reducing government growth, these changes in the programs would help to limit growth and reduce costs of employment programs in the long run. In sum, even though they were not designed to accomplish all three goals of contracting advocates, CETA goals were consistent with the desire for reduced costs, better services, and limited government growth.

Interviewee Selection

Two categories of individuals associated with the state CETA programs were selected for interviews—six state DOL officials in the Bureau of Employment and Training (BET), the unit responsible for the grants; and ten service providers. Of the BET employees, two respondents worked in the program and planning division, where they had responsibility for the early stages of the contract process—policy development, program design, and contract solicitations—as well as the design and implementation of any program evaluations. The four other BET interviewees were contract administrators. They negotiated contracts, assisted contractors, and monitored providers for contract compliance.

The ten contractor representatives were scattered throughout the state, but were located mainly in the same larger county areas where I had interviewed DSS contractors. Although no official permission was given (or necessary) to obtain these interviews, the BET interviewees provided complete lists of current and past CETA contractors. From these lists, I chose four agencies that had current contracts from BET for 1981, and six that no longer were receiving any from this source. More former contractors were interviewed than current ones (and more than in the DSS sample) because of the smaller number of current private contractors. Of the past contractors, I selected only agencies that had been awarded BET contracts within the past three fiscal years to avoid problems caused by staff turnovers, forgetfulness, or changes in the law.[16] About sixty percent of the current and recent private contractors were included in this sample.[17]

Backgrounds of Respondents

Except for one item, the backgrounds of both the public officials and the provider representatives were not unusual. They were not unlike those of the DSS interviewees, except that more of the interviewees (seventy-five percent) were women, compared to DSS (twenty-six percent). In addition, there did not seem to be the same movement between public and private agencies as was observed in the career patterns of the DSS interviewees. With two exceptions, the public sector work experiences of the private respondents were not in CETA-related organizations, such as DOL, BET, or local CETA prime sponsors. (Even these exceptions received their experience in other states.) Also, the actual interviews indicated that most, but not all, of the public respondents did not have as much knowledge and understanding of (or sympathy with) their private counterparts' positions. Their educational backgrounds may partially explain this; all but one of the public sector respondents had studied liberal arts and did not have degrees in the relevant professional fields of vocational education, adult education, manpower training, etc.

Contractor Agency Profiles

As with the DSS provider agencies, the ten BET contractors used in this study made up a diverse group of private, nonprofit agencies. Eight of the ten had contracts through the State Governors' Grants, Section 202 (e) (the four percent funds), that required direct service provision to CETA-eligible clients in certain target groups that had not been adequately served by prime sponsors—female offenders, women, adjudicated high school dropouts, Hispanics, the handicapped. The other two agencies delivered linkage and coordination services to CETA-related agencies under CETA's Section 202 (d) and (e).

Three of the six Title II contracts included in this sample were made with agencies that focused on women's employment needs, but were no longer in effect. The only current Title II contracts for direct client services were with an agency that offered pre-employment services for in-school youth, under three contracts totalling $626,352 for 1981. Two agencies provided special, non-client services for CETA-related bodies. One contract, implemented by the manpower section in the state office of one of the major unions in the state, was directed toward providing information on labor's role in CETA to prime sponsors and labor unions in various communities. The second contract was made with a small, new agency that delivered a variety of information and training services for staffs of Michigan prime sponsors. These two contracts were of particular interest since they were made because of the complexities of the CETA programs.

Of the four Title IV youth contractors, only one at the time of the interviews had a current BET contract (actually, for 1981, three contracts), totalling $179,354, for employment services for adjudicated high school dropouts. Two of the other agencies provided services for handicapped youth (and received a BET renewal later), while a third agency assisted Hispanic dropouts in finding employment. These programs were all located in certain designated communities and were not available to youth statewide, because they were for demonstration or experimental purposes.

The interviews with representatives of the ten contractors indicated that normally most of the agencies offered a wider range of services than just those purchased under the Governors' Grants. Their specializations and client groups differed widely as well, with the result that the agencies themselves were among the best experts on clients' needs, services, and appropriate methods of service delivery. The size of the agencies included in the sample ranged from five employees (a prison paralegal program for women) to over 200 (a migrant workers' agency). While two of the agencies had three BET contracts each for 1981, usually the agencies received only one contract—in amounts from $4,625 to $300,928. The age of the contractor agencies varied from a ninety year old YWCA to a new consulting firm. Most of the agencies were established since 1960 with government funds.

All of the contractors had a relatively low number of contracts (from one to five), but some of those contracts from other sources were for very large amounts. The state CETA contracts were usually not the largest of their government contracts. Several of the agencies had received CETA contracts from other government units—local prime sponsors, directly from the federal government—such that they could compare the BET contract procedures to other CETA procedures. Five of the agencies relied on government contracts for at least seventy percent of their operating costs, with some of these having no other sources of funds.

Unlike several DSS contractors, almost none of the DOL contractors seemed to be very dependent upon BET contracts, since they usually had a variety of public and private source of funds. In fact, two of the Title IV youth contractors did not request renewals after one year of a contract because of various bureaucratic requirements, rather poor results for clients, and the small amounts of the contracts, according to their representatives. In general, contractors understood that their BET contracts were for a three-year maximum period. (Only the union contract of $300,928 had been extended for a longer, indefinite time period. Two other current contractors expressed hope that theirs might be renewed after the three years, but they were not counting on it.) What appeared to be the case with these contracts was that they could be important for some agencies at the margins, since most agencies operate from hand to mouth, but contractors did not depend on them as their major funding source. Therefore, almost all of the agencies could survive without them.[18] In sum, the relatively small amounts of the contracts and BET's usual three-year limit apparently have helped to avoid the problems of dependence.

The only negative outcome of this lack of dependence seemed to be a less serious effort by some agencies at meeting BET's requirements and objectives—especially when they did not compare favorably with other governments' methods. One of the contractor interviewees said that the BET contract was so small that it was not worth their while to make a concerted effort at improving performance and 'putting up' with the hassles of the BET. Other contracts were more important to retain, and did not require compliance with as many difficult regulations. It appears that contractor dependence may have some advantages (as well as disadvantages) over contractor independence.

Conclusion

The major participants in DSS and BET contracting out were: first, the various officials in the state departments (and, in DSS, also the county offices) who were responsible for the planning and implementation of the contracts; and, second, the service providers who received the contracts and actually delivered the services to clients. The information, opinions, and viewpoints of these contracting actors will assist us in our examination of the conditions, process, and outcomes of human service contracting in Michigan. While the results of this study cannot be generalized to other states or other services, the use of major pieces of federal legislation and the comparison of the two different state contracting efforts should shed new light on the problems and possibilities of contracting out.

4

Competition in Service Environments and Contracting Procedures

When contracting out for goods or services is advocated, one of the main mechanisms for holding down costs and upgrading services is competition. Because the government agency should have more choice of supply than just its own bureaucracy, it can select the source that will most likely deliver what is desired at the least cost level. Yet the perspectives introduced in the second chapter challenge this assumption for economic, political, and administrative reasons. They suggest that the traditional economic doctrine about competition will not apply to contracting out, primarily due to the lack of responsive and responsible suppliers and the lack of desire or resources by officials to create competitive procedures.

The basic questions that need to be addressed are: To what extent are DSS' and DOL's service environments characterized by competition? and, Do the procedures used by contracting officials promote or hinder competition in the process? In this chapter, we will explore these issues, first, in DSS, and then in DOL. The conclusion analyzes the findings in terms of the theoretical perspectives to explain the lack of competition. By focusing on these issues, this chapter begins the task of assessing the presence of the three conditions outlined in the second chapter—competition, a rational decision making process, and government oversight of contractors' performance.

Competition in DSS' Service Environment

In general, few agencies competed for the contracts DSS could award. Except for two or three counties, receiving proposals from more than one or two agencies for a specified service was a rare occurrence. Some of the interviewees remarked that no other agency in the county or even in the state offered its kind of service (health services for migrant Hispanics, geriatric day care). Several reasons can be given for the small pool of available contractors for social services in Michigan. First, competition for clients and funding sources has not held a strong place in the tradition of the social services field. Public and private agencies have not considered themselves similar to profit-making enterprises, where the desire for profits and growth can encourage competition. Instead, social agencies have emphasized that their role is to serve people whose social and economic needs have gone unmet in a particular community. They differentiate their services and client groups from one another, to avoid direct competition and overlap.

Second, new or prospective contractors face barriers limiting market entry. For human service contracting, the market model is not particularly useful in understanding the buyers' role in purchasing services. Since they are limited in number and in purchasing range, government agencies act as monopsonistic or oligopsonistic interests—unlike the market model, where multiple consumers can allow for new firms and products to emerge to fill felt needs. In recent years, new private nonprofit agencies have been impeded from entering the social services market for the poor, unless they received a prior contract commitment from a government unit. Private funds are usually not enough for establishing an agency; even these sources often require a commitment from a public agency. The agencies that have been formed tend to be ones that fill an unmet need the government is especially interested in purchasing and have also found other funding sources. However, when the level of government funds is stable or declining, it is unlikely that government will purchase new services.

A good example of the problems involved in entering the social services market was provided by a new DSS contractor who operated a day care center for the elderly. Getting the DSS contract was problematic since the agency had no experience or track record in the field. The agency was awarded a contract only because the service was viewed as necessary for senior citizens, and no other agency could provide it. Obtaining additional funding from other sources was also very difficult, yet necessary, since DSS strongly encouraged it and any agency (whether established or new) usually required more than one funding source to survive. Thus, failure to gain the necessary funds and support from the community for a new program or agency can prohibit entry into the field, and thereby maintain a small pool of social agencies.

A third factor contributed to the lack of direct, service-by-service competition among social service providers for DSS contracts—locational limitations. Direct services depend on having a site that is relatively convenient to clients. For many agencies using a variety of experts and facilities, the option of having the agency operate in different locations in the state was not usually feasible. And county officials were hesitant to purchase services from an agency that did not have a base or office within the county limits, because they wished to make the service convenient to clients and they often wanted to support local agencies. Among the DSS contractors, only the money management firms established 'branch offices' in various counties in the state—largely because their service can be provided through a single counselor. As a result, there has been some competition among money management firms for DSS contracts. The alcohol rehabilitation center was also able to avoid this locational problem, because clients were sent to it from throughout the state. These alternatives have not been open to other providers, however. Each provider was usually limited to competing for contracts in one county. Consequently, small- and medium-sized counties, where only a handful of social agencies exist, have constrained contract choices.

A fourth reason for limited competition is that when the social service contracts became available through DSS during the late 1960s, not all social agencies were interested in them. In the past, providers offering services aimed at the special needs of the poor were few in number, because of limited funding sources and the difficulty of serving the needy adequately. Except for the religious organizations, most private agencies had middle class orientations for middle class clients. With the advent of the federal social services grants, many of these agencies were attracted by the available contracts, including Big Brothers and Big Sisters, family counseling programs, and agencies for the handicapped. However, for others, the funds have not provided a sufficient incentive for them to compete for DSS contracts, whether due to a lack of interest in serving the poor, present stable funding sources, or fear of being subject to numerous regulations.

In summary, competition among potential providers is hampered by barriers to entry into the 'market,' the locational limitations, the unwillingness of some agencies to compete for DSS contracts, and the differentiation in agency services.

The Donation Requirement

Although competition in the environment was minimal, the state and county departments could have adopted certain methods to encourage some limited competition for its contracts. But the regulations of Title XX and its predecessor as well as the state DSS were *not* designed to promote competition. The donation requirement was one of the primary ways by which competition, perhaps unwittingly, was hindered.

For each service, the Title XX grant required a twenty-five percent match from the state to receive the seventy-five percent federal funds. This stipulation was written to ensure that the state and local agencies should show some commitment to the services they chose to provide. In Michigan, some essential services had the match contributed by the state legislature (e.g., for protective services), or by county boards of commissioners for county programs. Usually, however, the requisite donation to the state was made by the very contractor that received a DSS contract.

Not only was twenty-five percent of the total amount of the contract supposed to be donated, but some of the Title XX regulations governing these donations helped certain types of agencies more than others. Public agencies were given preference over private agencies, and nonprofit providers were advantaged over proprietary firms. For public contractors alone, the regulations allowed in-kind 'donations' (e.g., office space, machines) to be made for almost all of the requisite match—only five percent of the contract amount was to be made in cash and actually sent on to the state government. All private agencies, however, were required to contribute twenty-five percent of the total contract amount in cash.

Obtaining the donation from the nonprofits for their contracts was also easier than it was from for-profit firms. The regulations forbade the direct donation of funds from proprietaries for contracts for which they were the recipients. If a profit-making agent was used, public officials had to find another donor (such as the county board of commissioners) or an intermediary who was willing to 'launder' the firm's donation. Both of these methods were time-consuming for contracting officials—and certainly did not encourage proprietary firms to compete. Adding to their problem was the acknowledged bias against for-profit agencies in the social services field. For two proprietary financial counseling firms that performed necessary services for DSS clients, the advantages of having the nonprofit status were so compelling that at the suggestion of state and county contracting officials, both formed and incorporated new nonprofit agencies to handle the DSS business.

One federal regulation about the donations was generally given only lip service in DSS. The regulation specified that if nonprofit agencies were their own donors, an 'independent decision' about awards had to be made—the donation was not to affect the choice of contractors. In the past, when federal funds exceeded DSS' ability to spend them, any agency that put up the donation was given a contract. These contracts were repeatedly renewed, with little scrutiny until the late seventies during the decentralization process. Even then, according to county contract coordinators, finding agencies with donations or outside donors was so difficult that competition was not increased and little changed in contract awards.

But the ability to make the donation for their contracts does not necessarily correspond to the ability to provide high quality, essential services at a reasonable cost level. Since some agencies did not have any 'extra' money to fund the match or were unable to arrange for an outside donor to make the contribution, they were not considered for awards. Consequently, providers with regular funds from an active solicitation program or other sources (e.g., religious organizations, foundation grants, United Way) were advantaged over agencies without these funding sources.

In at least one county, officials found an easy and inexpensive method to get around the donation stipulation. According to the coordinator, the salaries of contractor agency directors were sometimes 'inflated' to cover their donation. The county and the contractor agreed informally that the excess funds not actually paid to the director would be returned for the donation. Because donations could be made in quarterly amounts and the contractor could usually get an advance on the contract, the agency need not use any of its own money, or run into serious cash flow problems. Although I received no additional confirmation of this practice in other counties, the coordinator asserted emphatically that others used the same matching method. Thus, on some occasions, in effect, the federal government paid for the *entire* contract amount, instead of its usual seventy-five percent.

While most of the county officials complained about the difficulties of finding good suppliers that could also make the donation, the county board of commissioners in one of the larger counties fostered increased competition by supplying the local donation for many of its contracts. Consequently, almost twice as many contractors as usual submitted proposals for DSS contracts. Because of the increased competition, some of the previous contractors and several other reputable agencies were turned down for awards. The resulting dissatisfaction and ill will made the contracting officials' positions more difficult and uncomfortable. This example illustrates not only how critical the donation requirement was in reducing the pool of contractors in other counties, but it also shows that real competition may not be altogether desirable for participants.

Competition in DSS' Contracting Procedures

Government contracting procedures can enhance or inhibit competition among potential contractors as well as expand or reduce the range of choices for decision makers. The early steps in the contracting process are particularly crucial—the wide solicitation of potential contractors and the objective consideration of proposals (or bids, in other cases). Even though some of DSS' choice was limited by the social services environment and the donation requirement, some contracting procedures could be designed to allow contracting to simulate the marketplace. We need to examine if this occurs. Before this more detailed analysis is begun, however, a brief outline of the major steps of the contracting process is necessary. (They are simplified here, and did not always occur precisely this way, but they indicate the usual sequence.)

First, DSS officials in the counties and in the state program offices assessed clients' needs to determine the appropriate services to purchase. Next, the unit responsible for the contract, i.e., the contract owner, solicited public and private providers for proposals for the desired services. Once the proposals were submitted, various participants in the county or state DSS reviewed and evaluated them and made their recommendations. The county department head, with the advice of an appointed Board of Social Services, made the final decision for county contracts, while program division heads usually selected the state-level contractors, all subject to the signature of the state DSS director.

The selected contractor proposals were then sent to the DSS contract management division, where specialists reviewed the proposals and the budget for compliance with Title XX and state regulations. (Here or earlier in the process some changes in the proposals may have been made and agreed upon.) These individuals also drew up the contract documents, using a standard form (or 'biolerplate') prepared with the consent of the state attorney general's office. Finally, all the required signatures were obtained, and the contract year could begin.

In actuality, this entire process was time-consuming and complex, since many different offices and individuals were involved. Contracting officials worked on several contracts at one time, each with a great deal of paperwork that had to be processed according to standard procedures. When a local donation was required (as it was for all county contracts included in the sample), additional forms had to be drafted, and the donor included in various steps. The procedures were simplified a great deal, however, under three conditions: 1) when a wide solicitation was deemed unnecessary; 2) when the contractor acted as his/her own donor, and 3) when a contract was renewed in a similar form. Therefore, for bureaucrats at both state and local levels, strong disincentives existed to use contractors who could not contribute the twenty-five percent and to seek out new contractors.

Contract Solicitations

The solicitation stage is the most crucial phase in the contracting process, as far as competition is concerned. The historic requirements for competition in public purchasing for goods or services include the following: the presence of two or more available, willing, and responsible bidders; a complete, explicit, and realistic specification package that all interested parties can receive; the widest solicitation of qualified, potential contractors through the use of a bidders list; an atmosphere of objectivity and impartiality.[1] These requirements have been standards in the field, whether competitive bidding or competitive negotiations are used to make awards.

With the apparent motto of 'once a contractor, always a contractor,' the general rule at both the state and county levels was that the DSS solicited for proposals or program descriptions from more than one prospective contractor *only* when new money became available, as during contract decentralization. Even for new contracts, the number of potential providers invited to submit proposals was very limited, at least in part because of the lack of contractors in the service environment. Between one and ten community agencies (with the mode at approximately two) were contacted for each contract, depending on the service and the county's size.

Formal solicitation procedures and 'bidders lists' were seldom used by state and county offices. Solicitations were based on county staffs' knowledge of agencies and were fairly informal — a telephone call, word of mouth, a letter. The more formal and time-consuming Request For Proposal (RFP) process was not required by departmental policy, and, as a result, infrequently employed. In addition, since the mid-seventies, counties generally did not award contracts to agencies that submitted unsolicited proposals.[2] While not using the RFP format, most of the counties did send out more detailed explanations to those agencies that expressed an interest in a contract.[3] These packages seldom included the criteria by which proposals would be evaluated, or DSS' review methods during the life of the contract. In most cases, these procedures could be explained verbally either by the contract owner upon request, in a preproposal conference (if the county had one), or during contract negotiations.

All the counties and state program offices required a written proposal, including a line-item budget, before a decision was made on the contract awards. However, narrow solicitations produced few proposals for DSS consideration. In all but the four largest counties, receiving more than one proposal for a new contract was a rare occurrence. Therefore, in most counties, if it existed at all, the competition was not so much among agencies offering similar services that could be compared, but among dissimilar agencies all requesting a share of the county's allocation.

It is clear from this description that DSS' solicitation procedures did not foster competition. In addition, some of the county coordinators indicated they were not concerned about being impartial and objective in their relationships with potential providers prior to awards. Some suggested that the program staff also had their own biases in favor of certain agencies. The lack of formal solicitation procedures, solicitation criteria (i.e., determining who would be considered a responsible and responsive provider), and proposal evaluation criteria meant that personal judgments, prejudices, and oversights reduced the already minimal competition that existed in the social services environment.

Competition in the Employment and Training Environment

Our attention now turns to BET contracting to determine the similarities and differences in competition between the two human service cases. The employment and training field has been marked by only limited competition—and for some of the same reasons as were found in the social services: the need for providers to differentiate their services to enter the market successfully, locational restrictions, and government oligopsonies in the services market.

Employment and training services are clearly services that, prior to government articulation of demand, suffered from underexpression of demand and lack of adequate supply—even more than in the area of social services. When the federal government decided that this basic need of the poor should be met by government action, very few of the existing employment agencies or technical training schools offered their services. The government generally depended upon public agencies (e.g., public schools, public employment agencies) to accomplish its goals.

The public sector has remained the chief vehicle for delivery of manpower services to the needy, but some private agencies have been used. During the sixties, a number of private, community-based organizations (CBO's) created with federal grants developed expertise in various employment and training services. Though relatively few in number, these agencies became an important component of employment policies. When CETA brought almost all employment and training programs under the control of state and local public officials, and out of the hands of federal bureaucrats and nonprofit corporations, these agencies were able to gain enough political support in Congress to ensure the continued flow of funds. They received special considerations over other agencies under the CETA regulations—i.e., requirements that they be allowed to participate in the planning process, receive solicitations for contracts, and be awarded contracts where their programs demonstrated their effectiveness.

These regulations have not meant that CBO's and other private agencies have readily formed to compete with public agencies for state and local contracts, however. New private agencies (or existing social agencies seeking to expand their services) have experienced some difficulty more recently in entering the market to compete directly with public organizations for government funds, in part because of the government's oligopsonistic control over contracts. Some contractor interviewees complained they often were not seriously considered for local prime sponsor contracts because of longstanding loyalties to other related public agencies in the community. Private agencies included in this sample were able to form and continue with some success for at least one of three reasons: 1) they were local affiliates of national manpower networks (e.g., in youth employment—70,001 Ltd. and OIC, Opportunities Industrialization Centers); 2) they were successful in getting grants from private employers and/or the federal government directly (e.g., the migrant workers' organization); and/or 3) they entered the manpower programs as a by-product of some other primary activity in which they developed program or client expertise not found

64 CONTRACTING OUT FOR HUMAN SERVICES

in other private or public agencies (e.g., the labor union, rehabilitation agencies, YWCA). Generally, however, competition was discouraged in this field by the prime sponsors and the public agencies that received their contracts.

Reducing Competition Through BET Policy

The number of potential providers competing for CETA contracts was reduced further by one critical BET policy—the stipulation that a match for Title IV youth contracts be made during the second and third years of a contract. A match was not required by federal CETA regulations, but was designed by BET to achieve certain state goals. The three-year limit on almost all state CETA contracts may have in itself discouraged some providers from competing for contracts, but the matching requirement for the youth contracts went one step further; it allowed for only one year of being fully funded by CETA. For the second year, thirty percent of the amount had to be paid by the provider; in the third year, fifty percent. After three years, good programs were expected to have demonstrated their effectiveness and obtain a more permanent funding source to continue their services.

Thus, while discouraging dependence on BET contracts, the increasing match and the three-year limit also seemed to discourage especially private agencies with few outside sources of funds from competing for and/or renewing contracts. The three years of youth programs saw a decrease in the number of contracts with private agencies, since several agencies did not reapply for the second and third years. At the time of the interviews, none of the private contractors had continued for the full three years. One of the reasons given for this phenomenon was the matching requirement—some of the agencies had no extra money, while others had alternative sources available that did not require a match or complex regulations. Only two private agencies requested and received second-year contracts. The representative of one of these said that his agency's contract renewal was automatic because he had funds for the match. At this time, BET had little choice of contractors so it could not use the renewals as rewards for well-run, effective programs.

BET's experience with the Title IV match substantiates my earlier claim that a donation requirement reduces competition, especially among private agencies. DSS had difficulty finding agencies that could provide a particular service and also make the twenty-five percent donation. In BET, almost without exception, the Title II contractors requested the maximum number of contract years allowed by BET; Title IV providers opted out of their programs, and did not usually continue them with other funds. Therefore, the matching requirement not only reduced competition and choice, but sometimes did not allow promising programs to continue to the point of being successful and providing the unemployed with jobs—the very aim of the CETA grants.

Competition in BET's Contracting Procedures

All other things being equal, we would expect that the Title II funds would have encouraged more competition and choice for BET than the Title IV youth contracts because of the matching difference. The procedures for the two CETA titles were not, however, designed to be equally competitive. The Title II procedures usually produced limited competition, while the Title IV youth programs, at least for one year, created more competition and choice through the use of the RFP process.

Many of the procedures used by BET to purchase various services were governed by CETA regulations that generally emphasized the need for competition, objectivity, and fairness. Nonetheless, state governments could use their own discretion in choosing solicitation methods. Michigan BET used two different approaches to the two titles.

Solicitation Procedures

Unlike Title XX and the Michigan DSS, the goals of the state CETA titles and Michigan's DOL seemed to require competition in solicitation procedures to attract proposals for innovative projects that would most likely succeed. These CETA funds were not only to be spent to provide certain necessary services, but they were also intended for model and demonstration projects. Effective competition would seem to be the avenue to giving BET a variety of choices and achieving these goals. BET did not, however, consistently promote competition through its solicitation procedures. Major differences in methods were obvious between the Title II and Title IV contract process. Title IV contracting was marked by competition throughout the contracting process—at least for one year—but only minimal competition characterized the Title II process.

Although CETA regulations did not require it, BET used the RFP (Request For Proposal) process for the youth contracts in 1979, for the first full year of Title IV (FY 1980). It tried to achieve the widest exposure of the RFP by notifying approximately 600 potential public and private providers, including past contractors, prime sponsors, community-based organizations, and any agency that had expresed and interest in CETA contracts.

The contract specifications in the RFP were thorough and complete. Besides detailing the target population and service delivery requirements (both of which stemmed from previous needs assessments), performance goals were set (e.g., percentage of participants placed in unsubsidized employment) and prospective contractors were informed that they would be evaluated by BET for their goal achievement. Probably more importantly from the perspective of the contractors, the package clearly specified the proposals' evaluation criteria and their relative weight in the awards process. The RFP stated, for example, that extra 'points' would be given to proposals to enroll youths who met more than the minimum number of target characteristics.

BET did not use the RFP for the two following years of the youth grant (FY 1981 and 82), partially because the first solicitation had been so thorough and BET had not changed its goals for the grant. In addition, the process was very expensive, time-consuming, and complicated. Although this RFP process was a major undertaking, BET officials were not altogether pleased with its results—both in terms of the proposals received and the performance of the agencies awarded contracts. Of the 600 invitations, thirty-five proposals were received, of which sixteen were originally awarded contracts. These figures indicate some measure of competition; yet most of the youth proposals were judged as being poorly written, ill-conceived, and unresponsive to the department's needs. Despite some serious implementation problems as well, the funded agencies were invited to submit proposals for FY 1981 and then for FY 1982, provided they had not mismanaged funds or been found to be in "gross noncompliance" during the previous year. BET basically continued the previous year's contracts for contractors who requested them.

In contrast, the Title II solicitations were more similar to DSS' normal process. Except for a few specialized research and linkage contracts, the RFP was not used. Invitations to contractors were usually issued through informal contracts and letters. Some noncompetitive awards to public agencies have been used on occasion, as allowed by CETA regulations, but BET preferred to invite more than one contractor for proposals, since, in the words of one supervisor, "it could so easily be abused." Unlike the Title IV RFP process, Title II contract solicitation information was fairly brief and open-ended. Since the target groups, methods of service, and performance goals were not as precisely stated, providers proposed their own types of programs, the number and characteristics of enrollees, total cost figures, etc. Consequently, the process worked very much like the DSS system. Only a few proposals were received. Instead of achieving direct competition through wide advertising for certain specific programs, agencies submitted different types of proposals that could not be easily compared.

In contrast to the public agencies, most of the private agencies did not receive their Title II contracts through BET's solicitations; they contacted DOL first about funding for their programs. All four of the current and former direct service contractors reported that their agencies approached BET, rather than the reverse. Some interviewees suggested that BET had an inadequate knowledge of private agencies, such that public agencies were given preference in invitations. One respondent said that she had never seen any advertisements about the Title II contracts, even though she had been very involved in the employment and training policy field both in and out of Michigan for many years. This kind of bias meant that BET apparently failed to comply with the CETA regulation that community-based organizations be invited to participate, nor did it seek to promote competition in its Title II programs.

Conclusion

In this study, the lack of meaningful competition in the service market was a critical factor in limiting choices for both DSS and BET. Because of the small pool of willing, responsible, and responsive agencies, officials usually could not compare proposals, budgets, and performance for the same types of services. In addition, certain policies further reduced the choices for contractors. First, DSS' donation and BET's increasing match for Title IV obviously reduced the field of competitors and gave distinct advantages to certain contractors. Second, under DSS' decentralization, counties were usually restricted to purchasing from local agencies. In some counties, this meant that only some services could be arranged for delivery to clients. In contrast, BET had more choice of agencies from throughout the state, even though its efforts were often targeted at the major central cities. Third, the solicitation procedures have often not allowed for the widest exposure of the departments' contracts. Other, shortcut methods were easier and less costly for government officials than the major RFP solicitation for youth grants and the scattered cases of RFP's in social services.

Contracting in BET, however, has been marked by other procedures not found in DSS that have enhanced competition. The Title IV youth contract process was a model of wide solicitation to promote competition and choice, even if it did not achieve officials' hopes for well-written proposals. The RFP was viewed as necessary because of higher-level policy decisions of the increasing match requirement, the limit on the amounts of the contracts, and the prior specification of the method of service delivery and target groups. For these reasons and because a large number of new youth contracts were to be awarded at one time (originally sixteen), officials believed it would be easier and more productive to try the competitive RFP process. In addition, the three-year time limit cut two different ways in terms of competition. On the one hand, it probably made the BET contracts less attractive to prospective agencies; on the other hand, it may have widened officials' choices over time by preventing them from becoming locked into undesirable projects.

Since, in several ways, the competition condition of the public choice perspective was not fully realized in either DSS or BET, the three alternative perspectives must be examined to determine their relevance to the departments' potential pool of providers and their purchasing procedures. In this chapter, the perspectives of market imperfections and organizational decision making are particularly useful to this discussion of competition.

First, the market imperfections perspective predicted accurately that for some areas, such as social and employment services, the service environment would be characterized by insufficient suppliers to produce true direct competition. In these cases, however, the lack of competition is not so much due to the public good characteristics of the services (although they are certainly present), or the high capital costs associated with market entry, but rather because of the lack of economic resources of the poor. Low-income citizens cannot usually afford to purchase social and employment services; therefore, in the absence of government provision, their needs do not become demands in a marketplace that, not surprisingly, only responds to needs backed up by cash. Since there was no effective demand for these services until government stepped in, few agencies volunteered to provide them. When government agencies determined these services were essential to eliminating dependence on welfare programs, they had no ready source of expertise—neither in their own bureaucracy nor in the private sector. They had to create public and private agencies to supply the services. By so doing, however, state and local governments also created an oligopsonistic situation of a few buyers. This suppressed the emergence of new firms and agencies because agencies could not generally form and survive without a government grant or contract. The private agencies in this study were able to enter the social and employment services market when they had a prior commitment from a private agency; had a strong middle class, paying clientele; were affiliated with a national network of agencies; or provided their service only as a by-product of some other primary activity.

The organizational decision-making perspective also contributes to our understanding of the realities of DSS and BET contracting out. Not only did the officials have limited information about the service market, but they seldom used the RFP because it is expensive, time-consuming, and complex. The sequential search process (the incremental approach) usually was employed; decision makers retained previous services and contractors routinely, and only sought new alternatives when additional funds were allocated.

In many ways, this narrow search and lack of competition was mutually beneficial for most of the key contracting actors. Relying primarily on previous contractors reduces conflict about goals, produces predictable outcomes, and avoids delays. One of the primary concerns of almost all officials interviewed was to determine awards and process contracts in a timely manner with a minimum of confusion and controversy. The contracting process could proceed quickly and smoothly under the following conditions: when the contracting unit did not have to reach agreement on service priorities and proposal criteria; when an RFP and complete mailing list of suppliers was deemed unnecessary; when previous contractors made up most of the proposals; and when a thorough consideration of alternative proposals and agencies was not needed. When the fact of declining resources of personnel, time, and money is added to these disincentives for competition, is it any surprise that real competition among providers was the exception, rather than the rule?

Regular contractors did not welcome competition either, since they seek a stable, predictable source of funds. Writing good, competitive proposals is costly for organizations, particularly when a contract is not awarded for the effort. It is quite possible that some providers did not wish to submit proposals for programs when the solicitation was thorough and the competition would be stiff. The only actors who would have personally benefitted from competition were the agencies that otherwise would not have had an opportunity to compete, and the clients who might have received more necessary and/or better quality services as a result. Usually, however, these two groups were not active or organized participants in contract decision making, as the cooptation perspective reminds us.

5

Making Contract Decisions

Contracting advocates usually assume that decision makers will use outside agents to promote efficiency and cut the cost of government services. This assumption requires a rational decision-making process in which decision makers, for whatever reasons, try to maximize this goal by gathering sufficient information to predict the likely outcomes of various alternatives and by selecting the agency that most closely fulfills this goal. The three alternative perspectives, however, raise doubts that officials will adhere to this efficiency goal or that sufficient information will be obtained to make wise choices. To determine whose expectation is realized in DSS and BET contracting, decision making will be analyzed in three critical areas—first, in the decision to use outside suppliers; second, in the selection of services to be purchased; and third, in their choices of contractors. The history of social service contracting has already indicated that efficiency goals were not major considerations in the early years. But as Michigan found it increasingly difficult to stay within the state limit on Title XX allocations, did the DSS decision criteria change? Did decision makers in DSS and in BET try to get "the biggest bang for the buck?" Even if competition has not been a major ingredient in either service system, it is possible that participants would try to reduce costs and improve service delivery.

Why Contract Out for Title XX Services?

The decision to deliver services via contractors instead of in-house staff is a critical one in the contracting process. Using outside agencies would not be economically rational if this method was not expected to produce more efficient services. Yet DSS officials made it obvious that they did not periodically review the advantages and disadvantages of using contractors to deliver social services. Nor did they weigh the costs and benefits of in-house provision versus contracted services to make their supply choices. Instead, outside agencies were usually relied on because DSS caseworkers did not have the expertise to provide clients with certain services or programs. Even though they could have hired the necessary personnel, DSS believed it was both easier and better to use the existing, experienced agencies, particularly because of the donated funds and federal match. In the past, their decisions about purchase-of-services had been made because of the federal legislation and state pressures; changing priorities and traditional service agents in more recent times were considered very cautiously.

The twenty-three respondents associated with DSS services were asked to rank seven alternatives in order of importance as to why outside agencies instead of public employees were used to supply social services in their program area. (See Appendix B for interview schedule.) Although interviewees responded with various combinations, all three groups (state officials, county contract coordinators, and providers) selected the "better services" answer as the most important reason for contracting out. In fact, several stated that this was the *only* reason. By better services, they explained, not only could outside providers give generally better quality services than DSS caseworkers, but also that they had expertise in a wide range of specialized services clients needed. Without outside providers, DSS could not or would not have been able to provide the service at all (e.g., certain housing and money management services), or as well (e.g., health-related services for migrant workers).

Respondents were divided in their opinions about the additional reasons for contracting out. "Lower cost" was given by the contractors as their second reason, while officials ranked it third in importance. Interestingly, neither of the two provider spokespersons who had worked in the state DSS during the early seventies nor any of the veteran state officials chose this reason for their first or second choice. According to the more experienced bureaucrats, cost became more important in recent years, but was not a major reason originally for using private providers. Some respondents also made the essential point that the local donation made the services very attractive for the state government, since state funds were not expended. State and county officials' consideration of cost as a reason for using outside contractors, therefore, did not arise out of comparisons of DSS' and outside providers' total or per-unit costs of service (including both the federal and local amounts plus any other state-incurred expenses.) Rather, the calculated costs have been the costs to the *state* government, using the simple rule-of-thumb that donated funds services were virtually 'free' for the state. If provided through DSS caseworkers, the state itself would have had to contribute the match. Fiscal federalism removed some of the incentives to consider cost as a crucial factor in contracting—if, in fact, costs would otherwise have been a major consideration. Indeed, with the fixed size of the Michigan Title XX allocation shrinking under inflationary pressures, the contracted services looked like a relative bargain to a department that was having difficulty meeting the direct payment needs of its growing clientele.

Other answers of less importance were: "greater flexibility in hiring and firing" (especially for officials), "better oversight over cost and performance" (though not for state officials), and "a way of strengthening private agencies of firms" (of more importance to state officials). The alternatives of "political pork barreling" and "mandated by federal and state laws and regulations" were generally viewed as relatively unimportant reasons for contracting out. However, both of these reasons were critical, according to respondents, in sweetheart contracts, and certain money management and guardianship services that by law could not be performed by DSS employees. Two interviewees also commented that the politicians, federal regulations, and state policy encouraged contracting out under Title XX, but overall these encouragements were no longer viewed as significant as other reasons. Finally, one of the county services heads stated that contractors had been employed not only to provide a wide array of services for the poor, but also to expand the number of people in the community who had an investment in the public welfare, increasing the level of support for human services.

One of the problems raised by various public officials was the absence of an objective purchasing process in DSS. They complained that the state policy governing which types of services could or could not be bought was unclear, inconsistent, and subject to a variety of interpretations. As we will see, many of the counties have not conducted needs assessments or established service priorities. This lack of objectivity and a rational decision-making process was seen as too often creating problems in decisions about both contracting for services and making awards to providers. In addition, the county officials were particularly frustrated because of the lack of clarity about state and local roles in the contracting process. They were uncertain of who had responsibility for the various steps in the decision-making process.

DSS' Needs Assessments and Planning

In the early seventies, the usual procedure for deciding which services to purchase was to notify various public and private agencies about the available funds and the general regulations governing their use. Few attempts were made to assess clients' needs systematically, and then to solicit only for those high priority services. Consequently, many different service providers received contracts year after year with little review of needs, performance, or effectiveness. They frequently built up their agencies to accommodate the increased demand from government, and established good relationships with the relevant state bureaucrats and their legislators to ensure the flow of funds over time.

One of Title XX's major purposes was to establish a uniform and comprehensive process of planning for social services, in an effort to produce a more rational allocation of resources. Integral to this effort was the development of systematic needs assessments that included a greater opportunity for citizen participation. A needs assessment is "a process of gathering, ordering, analyzing, and presenting information about a particular problem or condition with the intent of influencing the allocation of resources committed to resolving or reducing the problem or condition."[1] Information about service populations, service needs, selection of an appropriate service mix, and the current supply of services by various agencies are all necessary components.[2]

When DSS decentralized some of the contract administration by designating counties as the contract owners with significant discretion, part of the rationale was that local DSS officials could conduct more manageable assessments and more adequately match local needs with local service providers. Although required by Title XX and stipulated in the central office's contract procedures, systematic needs assessments were not usually conducted and only occasionally were they used to determine service needs—and then generally in the counties that had new money to purchase new services.

When used, the assessments were hardly systematic and thorough. They usually depended upon two major sources of information and input—DSS caseworkers and local social agencies (many of which already had contracts). Generally, clients' service needs were only *indirectly* measured—filtered through participants in the social services system who had particular interests in the outcome. In turn, these reports were interpreted by the local DSS officials involved in contracting—program heads, contract coordinators, department directors, the social services boards, and sometimes, the county boards of commissioners.

In one case, a provider asserted that the process of determining needs priorities was biased. His agency formerly had a family counseling contract with the state DSS, in part because of political pressure by a statewide agency association. During the life of the state-awarded contract, he complained to officials that the county DSS workers were not making referrals to his agency, as specified under the terms of the contract. Then after contract decentralization, the agency failed to get a renewal at the county level, according to the agency director, due to "political" reasons—the local DSS staff "didn't want a successful agency to show that it can do counseling better" than DSS caseworkers. The county discontinued the purchase of counseling services altogether because, they said, this service was being performed by DSS in house, and the overlap was unnecessary. This change of contractors occurred in the county mentioned in the previous chapter, where the competition for contracts was increased by the board of commissioners contributing the match. As a result, county officials had a greater choice of agencies from which to purchase services.

In addition, the state DSS' allocations of Title XX funds for county donated funds were not based on any formula of needs and population. Instead, funds were distributed on the basis of previous purchase levels. In other words, if a county had purchased many services early on in the decentralization process, it continued to receive more contract staff positions and federal funds to match than a similar county that had not purchased as much at that time. For example, Ingham County (pop. 275,000) received larger allocations than both Kent County (pop. 433,000) and Genesee County (pop. 442,000, with far greater welfare needs, particularly in the city of Flint). In FY 1979-80, Ingham County was allocated $434,150, while Genesee County received $429,457 and Kent County got only $228,517. Several contract coordinators complained about this method. According to DSS written policy, the state DSS' goal was "to eventually have donated funds allocated to local offices based on measures of social service needs."[3]

Choosing DSS Contractors

The usual process of evaluating contractor proposals in the counties involved four major groups of officials: the county DSS staff, the county board of social services, the county department director, and the state DSS officials—especially those in the program and contract management offices. Since these participants had differing goals and perceptions, and since the multiple decision points were designed to check contract choices, the process was often lengthy and sometimes conflictive. State officials provided guidelines, assistance, and oversight during the early stages; they processed forms and monitored contractor compliance during the contract's life. The various county officials were given the task of making awards to contractors. But who in the county was actually most influential in the selection varied from county to county, and under decentralization the responsibilities of the state versus the county offices were quite unclear.

In the first step of the selection process, the county contract coordinator, his/her supervisor (e.g., service head, deputy director), and relevant program heads were to make their recommendations after reviewing the proposals for "completeness, specificity of the program description consistent with local office needs assessments, reasonableness and if within the State Plan and Federal goals."[4] If a proposal contained questionable elements, the proposing provider was brought in to negotiate or revise them. In many cases, the contractor was the expert concerning the cost of various items or elements, which program elements were essential, what was practicable, etc. The public officials had few means of comparison and seldom sought outside sources of information. As a consequence, the original proposal form was usually not altered significantly.

Next, the social services board examined the proposals and stated their preferences of providers. Each county had a three-member, voluntary board, with two members appointed by the county board of commissioners, and the third by the governor. These individuals were generally civic or business leaders who had an interest, but not necessarily any expertise, in the social service field. The board's normal role within the department was an advisory one; it reviewed, recommended, and commented on the range of policies, programs, and problems in the county DSS. The board also had the authority to examine all DSS contracts to ensure that they conformed to state statutes and Title XX (under Michigan Public Act 237 of 1975).

Their actual role in contract decision making apparently depended upon the individuals themselves, their role perceptions, the use the department directors made of them, and the ability of the staff to 'manage' or influence them. In some counties, the boards were described by interviewees as rubber stamps of the decisions made by influential contract coordinators or service heads. In others, respondents expressed some frustration about the boards' decisions since they had not always agreed with staff recommendations. For example, one county's coordinator reluctantly went along with the board's suggestion to solicit more widely for another money management firm, but felt that the current, local contractor should have his contract renewed. The board decided instead to award the contract to an outside firm that had several branch offices in the state. This action angered the coordinator largely because the change involved much additional work for her.

The county department director had final authority on awards (subject to the signature of the state DSS director). It depended upon the individual, the department, the board, and sometimes outside political forces as to whose recommendations for awards were actually approved. Some directors took an aggressive role in making these decisions, while others approved the decisions made by key staff members and/or the board. The usual strategy of directors appears to have been to gain staff and board consensus. Conflict could best be avoided if none of the participants wished to alter the current services and providers. If a change was suggested, it was likely to be resisted by other participants and, obviously, the contractors and their allies. Officials had few inducements and several constraints involved in changing the status quo.

This preference for avoiding change was revealed in officials' answers to this question: "On what basis is it decided that a certain firm or agency will receive a contract in your program area?" State and county officials chose three major reasons, in the following order: previous satisfactory work in state services, adequate staff and equipment, and experience in this general type of service. Lowest cost, a plan to fulfill all criteria provided in the solicitation package, political influence, and well-reasoned arguments why program elements would accomplish the desired goals were mentioned, but infrequently. Many of the respondents found this question difficult to answer, since a variety of criteria was used, depending upon the service, the officials involved, and the availability of providers.

Most of the public officials indicated that frequently they had few real choices—previous contractors got renewals and new contracts were awarded to the only available, reputable agency in the community equipped to handle the service and capable of supplying the donation. The more critical choice for small- and medium-sized counties (and often even the state program offices) was in deciding which service to purchase, since it in turn determined the supplier. The reputation and operation of the agencies influenced this selection of services. Often the two different decisions about service needs and contract awards were essentially combined into one.

Contractor representatives chose a somewhat different set of reasons for awards, in order: experience in this general type of service, political influence, previous satisfactory work in state services, and lowest cost. These were the contractors' *perceptions* of award criteria, rather than the more direct observations made by the public officials. As for the lowest cost choice by contractors, they explained that they were impressed by DSS' request to cut back during the latest round of contract negotiations. However, the bureaucrats made it clear that usually cost level or per-unit costs were not a major criterion for awards. Contractors also selected the political influence response more often than bureaucrats, perhaps because some had had more direct experience with political awards, or because they overstated the influence of politicians in the process; it is possible, however, that the officials might be somewhat hesitant to admit that politics was an important factor in their profession.

Reasons for Lack of Objectivity and Fairness

It was apparent in the last chapter that DSS' solicitation methods were not aimed at increasing competition, fairness, and objectivity. The award process did not promote these goals either. Officials did not necessarily choose services and providers on the basis of lowest cost with the best quality services. In general, the agencies usually chosen for contracts were ones that, in the opinion of decision makers, would supply good quality services for clients and were able to work well with DSS officials. Comparing the costs of various services and agencies was rarely done, due to the difficulty of measuring and comparing costs and benefits of very different programs, the lack of choice among providers, and the failure of officials to make decisions on the basis of cost. In one case of competition between two money management agencies, the county board of social services and the staff recommended that the agency proposing the lower cost with essentially the same services *not* be granted a contract. They chose the other, more experienced agency because they believed its cost figures were more realistic, given the requisite quality of services.

Some of the service and award decisions were strongly criticized by state program and contract management officials. One official, with a business background, complained that it was difficult to get the program and county staffs to act like they were *buying* services, instead of funding them. A program head said that "some counties are too heavily involved in facilitating friendships instead of the program goals" that were set by the program offices. He and other state officials questioned some of the awards made by some counties (e.g., choosing Dale Carnegie, Inc. to teach General Assistance clients how to improve themselves by winning friends and influencing people). Moreover, according to DSS officials, too many of the counties (and some state programs) became 'locked into' certain older contracts, such that they did not purchase the best quality and most necessary services for clients.

Part of the explanation for some dissatisfaction with the choices was due to DSS decision-making procedures. First, the identities of the proposers were known to all contracting participants. As a result, factors besides the proposal could affect the decisions, including prejudices against certain types of agencies (e.g., proprietaries), knowledge of political connections, personal feelings about individuals associated with the agencies, etc. County officials naturally defended this practice, since they believed it was essential to know the reputation of the agency and its previous experience. If a 'blind' evaluation had been required, in all but the largest counties, most of the officials would have known who submitted which proposals nonetheless. Second, most of the counties did not establish and disseminate their selection criteria. Different participants could use a variety of criteria, some of which may have had little relevance to client needs, costs, and service quality. In writing proposals, therefore, providers operated in the dark concerning the needs and expectations of DSS, unless they had access to inside information. Indeed, it was advantageous to the contractors, then, to try to facilitate good personal relationships. Third, DSS' monitoring and evaluation procedures have not served to assist decision makers, as we will learn in the next chapter. Interviewees suggested that they were often hindered in decision making because they lacked adequate information about the programs' effectiveness. Officials had to rely on providers' own cost figures and performance measures, since they did not have the resources or inclination to verify the information included in the proposals.

Relationships Between Bureaucrats and Contractors

Thus far, the pattern of decision making on DSS contracts is clearly at variance with that assumed by the public choice school's contracting out proponents. Often the goals and the contracting procedures of DSS officials were not oriented towards the pursuit of cost savings for government. It is not surprising then that some decision makers also allowed their personal relationships with providers and/or political pressures to influence their choices. For the most part, the professional bureaucrats disapproved of these influences, but recognized that these factors sometimes have determined final decisions. They were less aware, however, of their own biases and those of the program staffs.

To examine the types of relationships that were built up between the public contracting agents and private contractors, respondents were asked two questions. The first was:

> Use the following terms to describe your own relationships with contractors/public officials in your area of contracting:
> 1. close and personal
> 2. warm and friendly
> 3. strictly business like
> 4. cool and distant
> 5. hostile and antagonistic

They were given a frequency rating scale from one through four (always, often, sometimes, or never) to indicate how often their relationships could be characterized in the five above ways.

Interactions between bureaucrats and providers were often warm and friendly, as described by most state, county, and contractor respondents (83 percent, 71 percent and 80 percent, respectively). For some individuals, however, relationships were not always harmonious. At least three people in each group stated that their dealings were sometimes cool and distant, or hostile and antagonistic. Two newer contractors and the two providers who had not had DSS contracts renewed reported these less-than-friendly relations. Although the civil servants more frequently said that interactions were strained at times, it did not necessarily mean that they had a more negative view of working with contractors. These officials probably had more problems because they were given the unpleasant tasks of hearing complaints, reprimanding unsatisfactory providers, and trying to explain why contracts were late, reduced in amounts or not renewed. The last contract cycle in particular had taxed the county coordinators, since contract payments were delayed and cut due to the state's fiscal crisis. They, rather than the state officials, acted as the buffer between the contractors and the state DSS.

The second question was designed to ascertain if bureaucrats felt they acted as advocates for contractors, and if contractors perceived them doing so. A bureaucratic advocacy role would conform to the cooptation perspective on public/private relations. State and county interviewees were asked:

> How frequently do you see yourself acting as an advocate for service providers in your work (e.g., as with other state officials)?

Contractors were given this version:

> How frequently do you think that the service contract coordinator(s) in the state/county acted as an advocate for your agency and other service providers (e.g., as with other state officials)?

All were provided with the same four-part frequency scale (always, often, sometimes, never).

All but one of the six county contract coordinators or service supervisors indicated that they always or often acted as advocates for contractors. Not surprisingly, they reported this more frequently than did the state officials (only half of whom gave these responses), since the latter were further removed from most contractors. As part of their advocate role, county officials stated that they presented contractors' demands to other officials, as well as advocated the use of outside agencies to supply services.

The provider representatives apparently did not see these officials acting on their behalf as frequently as officials reported. The majority (or six out of nine respondents) said their coordinator only sometimes advocated their positions with others. (The one contractor who responded with 'always' to the question had been employed in her agency for only a few months and previously had worked in contract policy for the state DSS, so she may not have had the same kinds of experiences as other providers.)

From these answers and their comments, I concluded that most, but not all, of the state and county officials tried to help contractors through what can only be described as a "huge bureaucratic maze" (to use one interviewee's words), but without taking on the role of promoting the causes of their agencies when unwarranted. While sympathetic to the needs of contractors, they were critical of some who had not performed well and those who tried to work the system to their own advantage (e.g., those who tried to mobilize political support to prevent funding loss). Contractors, therefore, could not assume that these officials would be their allies.[5] It is probably healthy that contractors did not see their bureaucratic contacts as always acting on their behalf. They would be more likely to perform better if they were somewhat uncertain about the friendship or advocacy role of officials.

On the other hand, not all county contracting officials kept a distance between themselves and contractors. In two of the counties, I found evidence that the relationships were cooptative, instead of objective. These county officials were anxious to defend their contractors versus the state DSS; they worked at promoting cooperative, rather than competitive, relationships; they spoke in very favorable terms about their agencies and the need to keep them going; and they seemed to trust their contractors implicitly. They did not see the need to have thorough reviews of performance — only enough to show others that they were doing their jobs. While I could draw this conclusion only for those counties where interviews were conducted, I could conjecture from state-level interviews that a few of the other counties also fit this pattern. It should be stressed that the incentives to produce such cozy relationships were high: officials had to work constantly with their contractors; they desired cooperation, not conflict, to accomplish the state's requirements; they often had similar training and work experiences that produced sympathy for private agencies; and to receive positive work evaluations, they needed the support of the agencies. Therefore, the traditional accountability mechanisms in the system were critical in contracting decision making to check abuses resulting from these relationships.

Politicians and Politics in DSS Contracting

Although previous questions did not show that political pork barreling and pressures were very important factors in contract decisions, several of the respondents made vague or disparaging comments about the role of politics in the process. To assess more directly how politicians got involved, and how the respondents reacted, the following question was asked:

> In your experience in contracting, how do you evaluate the role of most politicians (e.g., state legislators, county commissioners, city councilmen) in the contracting process?
> 1. generally quite helpful
> 2. not involved enough in contracting
> 3. too interfering in decision making
> 4. hardly involved at all, but that's the way I prefer it
> 5. only involved in contracts that their constituents want, but otherwise hardly involved at all
> 6. some other response(s)

Their responses indicated that politicians, especially state legislators and county commissioners, could and did exert some pressure on contracting officials, although not in all counties. This was not uniformly perceived in negative ways by interviewees, however. In fact, several persons said that politicians were generally quite helpful. A county contracts coordinator added they could act as a check on the DSS administration in specific instances where otherwise important factors would not have been taken into account in decisions. Some providers mentioned that occasionally they had contacted their representatives and found them to be helpful.

None of the respondents believed that the elected officials were not involved enough in contracting affairs. Five respondents said that the politicians were hardly involved at all, but they preferred it that way. According to nine interviewees, when elected officials did get involved, they usually acted on behalf of constituent providers' interests, and not those of DSS' clients or the general public (as in having an interest in contracting procedures or costs). Public and private respondents did not always see the politicians' role as a healthy one. One official asserted that they were too interfering at times, while another stated that local politicians represented only the interests of friends and relatives.

Both providers and officials told of cases where certain decisions were influenced by politics. Two of the providers who were interviewed had been pointed out by officials or by themselves as being the recipients of sweetheart contracts made as the result of a special political relationship with the state DSS director and/or a powerful state representative. (One of these was no longer a true sweetheart, since it received more scrutiny after DSS' decentralization. The director said his agency kept getting contracts only because of inertia.) Such contracts were the exception, most interviewees affirmed, but they irritated the contracting officials nonetheless, because they believed another agency could have performed better, or because another service was more necessary to clients. A state program head was particularly angry at the state legislature as a whole, since for two years, it required DSS to purchase pregnancy counseling services from a private anti-abortion agency, against the desires of her office and the department. This situation was part of the ongoing tug-of-war between the state legislature and the governor over the funding of abortions for low-income clients.

The county boards were also influenced by politics, in part because of the appointment process. On occasion, partisan conflicts erupted in Democratic counties where the county board of commissioners appointed two of the three members, while Republican Governor Millikin chose the third. One of the providers complained of 'rampant politics' in one of the counties where he had lost a contract. In this unusual case, the board decided to make only one contract with a senior citizens agency instead of dividing up its allocation, largely due to the active lobbying of the elderly. The contractor believed the poor had a greater need for a range of services (including his money management), but they were not vocal or organized.

In sum, elected officials did have a role in various contract decisions throughout the seventies. On occasion, they influenced contracting officials to make choices they otherwise would not have made. Because some providers and their constituencies established strong ties with influential politicians and appointed officials, it was often difficult to reduce or eliminate certain services and providers when the staff believed a change was warranted. This political muscle was not flexed often, but contracting participants understood its potential power—and, therefore, acted with caution in suggesting changes. It is not surprising that almost all 'old' contracts were routinely renewed in the counties and at the state program level. The ones that were eliminated or reduced were usually with providers who did not have bureaucratic or political allies in key positions. The political pressure that could be exerted served to strengthen the position of most current providers. In addition, it reduced the fairness and objectivity in the system, and may have prevented some potential contractors from participating. It acted as yet another constraint upon contract decision making to narrow the range of choices that could be considered.

Why Contract Out for CETA Services?

Our attention turns again to the case of BET contracting out. As with DSS, BET's reasons for using outside agencies were not based on inherent cost and service advantages. Rather, the underlying reason for using outside agencies for CETA programs was that BET lacked the staff and facilities to implement the mandated and optional programs. The intention of the state titles, in addition, was to encourage states to use the existing local prime sponsors, school districts, community-based organizations, etc. for innovation, coordination, experimentation, and the targeted services. Consequently, relatively few activities (and rarely client programs) were produced by BET in house.

Therefore, the interview schedule's question about why outside agencies were used to supply CETA services took some respondents by surprise.[6] Although a few had difficulty answering, the public officials chose the "greater flexibility" alternative most frequency. "Better services" also appeared as relatively important, in the sense that outside agencies had expertise in clients and services not available in BET. Somewhat less significant were the "lower cost" and "better oversight" options. While two officials stated that contracting out was a way of strengthening private agencies, others disagreed and said that was not a reason. Two comments given as other key reasons were: "it makes no sense to have a statewide, state-level program for local problems," and outside agencies "happen to be available and can do it well."

Not surprisingly, the private agency representatives most frequently chose the "better services" alternative, or "greater flexibility in initiating and terminating programs," in the words of a respondent who improved on my wording. Unlike the officials, they believed that federal and state mandates were instrumental in the decisions. Of somewhat less importance were lower cost, better oversight, and a way of strengthening private agencies. Political pork barreling, with one exception, was seen as irrelevant to the decision to use outside suppliers.

BET used contracting out in part because it lacked the requisite expertise and organization to carry out the programs. Contracting with established agencies afforded greater flexibility than organizing a new agency. Probably more critically, purchasing services meshed with BET's (and CETA's) version of administrative decentralization—i.e., local agencies should be given contracts that could be continued through local support. In recent years, as Michigan's resources became increasingly limited and social needs grew, contracting proved to be an even more desirable alternative. The federal funds were available, but the state government imposed periodic hiring freezes, cutbacks for state travel, and finally, personnel cuts that affected only in-house supply. For the most part then, the early and more recent benefits of outside supply arose from the accompanying organizational policies and pressures—*not* necessarily from cost and service quality advantages.

BET's Needs Assessments and Planning

The Bureau of Employment and Training had several ways to determine the services to be purchased by Title II and IV funds—CETA mandates, informal and formal needs assessments, planning task forces, and Requests For Proposals. Under CETA, the state had specific responsibility for the employment and training needs of institutionalized individuals. In addition, BET used several advisory and information sources to determine if the prime sponsors were meeting the specific needs of certain client populations. They included the prime sponsors themselves; the Michigan Employment and Training Council (METC), a large, CETA-mandated advisory body consisting of interested experts and individuals; the CETA management information system, which produced a great quantity of employment data, including the type of services available and enrollments for various populations throughout the state; and the monthly reports of the DOL affirmative action officer, who analyzed the distribution of services for various groups. The planning and program half of BET used this information to select target populations and programs that coincided with CETA guidelines.

In 1979 and 1980, BET established two planning task forces when it became apparent that older workers and handicapped individuals had special needs that had gone unmet. Each task force was an ad hoc committee consisting of representatives of these groups, providers, and prime sponsors. With their input about employment needs and programs, BET intended to fund a few local demonstration projects for the next fiscal year. These and other efforts at assessing needs and suggesting possible providers appeared to promote a necessary balance between the objectivity of the research components and the responsiveness to concerned individuals and groups.

The more recent Title IV youth grant planning process largely depended on research that showed that certain subgroups among unemployed youth needed additional employment assistance: physically and mentally handicapped, racial minorities, heads of households, adjudicated youth, high school dropouts, central city and rural residents. The program staff drew up an RFP specifying that contracted projects should serve youth with some of these characteristics. In addition, it required that all the projects should include at least on-the-job training (OJT), since the research results convinced officials that OJT was the best method of ensuring that enrollees would continue in unsubsidized employment.

Not all the BET contracts used such systematic means for determining needs, however. In previous years, the target populations and service delivery methods were not as well-defined in advance of the solicitation stage for the service contracts. Instead, program officials had general ideas that more projects for certain groups (e.g., women) were needed, but did not pinpoint programs or subgroups to develop. Instead, the contracts often resulted from the proposals that agencies submitted—either in response to a general invitation or through their own initiative.

Choosing BET Contractors

Not only did the solicitation procedures for the two CETA titles differ, as was seen in the previous chapter, but the two processes of evaluating proposals also were very dissimilar in BET. The methods for judging the Title II proposals were frequently almost haphazard, while the Title IV process was fair and systematic for the most part. Common to both titles, however, was a general concern for the proposed program, the methods of service delivery, and needs of the targeted clients.

The Title II proposals were almost always evaluated by relevant program staff on their individual merits in light of the needs of the client groups and the available funds. Contracts were frequently considered and written throughout the year, such that all proposals were not compared to each other simultaneously. Usually the officials knew the identities of the providers. Their recommendations were then given to the bureau and department directors for their scrutiny and final decision. In the FY 1981 proposal considerations, all the agencies that submitted proposals or letters of intent received contracts, several of which were renewals. In previous years, roughly half of the unsolicited and solicited proposals were selected for contracts. Nonetheless, those agencies proposing specialized programs and target groups met little direct competition. All of the Title II contractors interviewed suggested that no other agencies in Michigan could supply their kinds of employment and training services for their client groups. Like DSS, if BET received more proposals than could be funded, the bureau determined contracts mainly on the basis of the target groups and proposals—not necessarily which contractor had the best project and success rate.

A more complex and objective process for considering proposals was employed when the RFP was used for the Title IV youth contracts. (It was also used a few times for Title II when several research proposals were submitted for a smaller number of contracts.) A panel of disinterested reviewers was chosen from among prime sponsor representatives, selected members of METC (Michigan Employment Training Council), and BET staff members (not including those who had written the RFP or who subsequently wrote and monitored the contracts). This panel examined and scored each proposal according to the RFP's written criteria; discussed top contenders when scores were close; and, presumably without knowing proposers' identities, recommended that the top scorers be awarded contracts. While these recommendations usually determined the outcomes, again both the bureau director and the department director made the final selection.

To determine if officials really followed this process, interviewees were questioned about the criteria used in award decisions. Their answers generally verified the description above, with the two major reasons for BET's choices being "a plan to fulfill all criteria provided in solicitation package," and "well-reasoned arguments why program elements will accomplish the desired goals, as given in the proposal." Other reasons mentioned were "previous satisfactory work in state projects or services" and "previous experience in this general type of service." Interviewees agreed that lowest cost was not a factor in decision-making. However, one of the respondents who made the award recommendations to the bureau director stated she wished the only reasons for choices were the first two mentioned above. From her vantage point, she saw that political factors were also important once the final decisions were in the hands of the bureau director and the department director, since they sometimes changed the awards.

The provider respondents said that they were uncertain concerning the reasons for awards, and their answers confirmed this. In this respect, the providers were generally less informed than DSS providers, who may have understood the system better because of long-term relationships with officials. (Many of the BET contractors were also very mistaken about the identities of those who selected contractors.) Their answers generally stressed the importance of their service experience, rather than the two primary reasons given by officials. This difference in responses between the two groups may indicate that providers often did not know what BET wanted and may explain why BET was disappointed with the quality and content of many proposals. Although some believed that costs were a consideration, interestingly, none of the contractors mentioned that political influence was a factor. In fact, some of the interviewees stated that compared to the favoritism in the awards of prime sponsors, the state BET appeared to be remarkably free from politics. The only complaint in this regard was that public agencies seemed to be preferred in the solicitation process.

Once the providers were selected, the specialists in contract administration were given the responsibility of negotiating and drawing up the contracts, as well as providing technical assistance during the projects' start-up period. Only here were the costs of the programs discussed—*after* the awards were made. The administrators examined contractors' budgets and, if necessary, suggested ways to change the line-items or program details to comply with the many complex CETA regulations. In the past, some agencies selected for awards were unable to complete the contracts during the writing stage because of noncompliance. One of the major problems in this phase was that the program and planning side of the bureau was primarily concerned with the programmatic elements of proposals, with the result that contractors were unaware of the many restrictions and paperwork required until later. Some insurmountable technical problems emerged only when the contract administrators took over in the process. When contracts could not be written, the funds were given to the next highest scorer in the Title IV 'contest,' another Title II contractor had to be found, or other contracts were given increases. For the youth contracts, sixteen of the providers were originally chosen for awards, but because of nonconformance with CETA regulations, two providers were eliminated. By the time that all avenues for resolving the problems had been exhausted, the contract year had already begun and it was too late to select replacements, with the result that the money was redistributed.

Judging from the evidence, officials' avowed purpose was to maximize service performance instead of cost reduction or efficiency. Awarding contracts to providers with good proposals for programs aimed at the most needy was BET's method for achieving this goal. This meant, however, that often BET evaluated potential contractors on the basis of limited information—information compiled by providers themselves almost exclusively about the program's clients, elements, service delivery approach, etc. In particular, four problems with this approach were apparent: 1) information (including reputation, past performance) about the likelihood of attaining program objectives was not used in either the Title II or IV award process; 2) since contract administrators were not consulted for their evaluations of new proposals or renewals, decision makers made their choices with limited knowledge of how well providers could operate their projects in accordance with CETA regulations and goals; 3) proposal evaluators often did not have independent information or expertise with which to judge the practicability and expected success of specialized proposals about clients and services (e.g., paralegal services for incarcerated women); and 4) there may not have been any necessary connection between the ability to package a credible program and being able to implement the plans, since often these two activities require different skills.

Besides having inadequate information, BET had some additional problems in accomplishing its goals for successful programs, particularly in the youth grant. Because of the realities of the bureaucratic environment, even though officials judged many of the proposals to be inadequate, all the Title IV funds were allocated. An official who was responsible for the RFP and proposal evaluations declared that if she had had a choice, she would have only purchased services from two or three of the thirty-five agencies that had submitted proposals, instead of the sixteen originally granted contracts. Another program official stated that BET "becomes more and more pressured as time goes on, because the money is ready to spend"; and had to go "with less than adequate plans." In the youth grant case especially, officials operated within severe time constraints, since each step of the RFP process was so time-consuming. BET also tried to assist contractors in improving their plans, meaning the entire contract writing process was delayed a full three months. Since the administrative system offered no incentives to states or officials who returned unused appropriations, the contracts were awarded to some private and public agencies that were unlikely to produce well-run, effective programs.

Not surprisingly then, BET's competitive procedures and impressive aims did not lead to good quality, effective service performance either. Once funded, some of the projects experienced late starts, inadequate record-keeping systems, and/or difficulty in meeting other contract terms, including the performance goals for placing enrollees in unsubsidized employment. Various reasons were given for the failures besides contractors' inadequacies, including the state of the economy, slow processing by BET, and unrealistic expectations of the program officials. After the first year, almost all those who requested them, received renewals, despite the difficulties. One of the contractors stated that the youth program placed a "heavy weight on intent and design, no so much on success."

The advantage of granting renewals was that the various start-up problems associated with an experimental project and a new funding source might be overcome with additional time, experience, and technical assistance from BET. Therefore, giving renewals may have helped to accomplish BET's goal of establishing model programs that later could be supported by local funds. Yet throughout the interviews, officials and contractors did not emphasize so much the need for program success as good program design and smooth operations.

Objectivity and Fairness in BET Contracting

The complex CETA regulations included several provisions for promoting fairness in contract decisions. Political patronage and conflict of interest in awards, for example, were strictly forbidden. Although certain types of contractors (CBO's) were to be given 'maximum reasonable opportunity' to compete and receive awards, and public agencies and prime sponsors were given some edge in solicitations, generally the selection of contractors was to be made on the basis of merit after a thorough review. In most respects, these regulations appear to have been followed in Michigan BET. The awards process was intended to be fair and objective, and relationships between the contracting officials and bureaucrats appeared to be more objective than those in DSS. As mentioned above, however, politics was a factor in some awards. In the next sections, we will examine the causes of both objectivity and political favoritism.

Relationships Between Bureaucrats and Contractors

To examine the associations among contracting participants, I asked respondents to rate the frequency (always, often, sometimes, or never) of "close and personal," "warm and friendly," "strictly businesslike," "cool and distant," and "hostile and antagonistic" relationships. Officials described their relationships as either often warm and friendly or strictly businesslike. Very few differences in perceptions between officials and contractors were evident, although BET officials stated somewhat more frequently that their relationships were sometimes cool and distant or hostile and antagonistic.

When asked about bureaucrats' advocate role, contract administrators, more than program officials, saw their jobs in terms of assisting their contractors, e.g., clearing payments for them, promoting their programs with other officials, finding their way through BET's confusing policies and bureaucracy. As in DSS, those who worked closely with the contractors were more likely than others to state that they always or often acted as an advocate. For the providers, the responses were more scattered across the choices. Their answers seemed to depend in large measure on the contract administrator assigned to them, since some administrators took on the advocacy role more frequently and were generally more cooperative than others. Unlike in DSS, where none of the providers chose 'never' for this question, three of the respondents said officials never acted as their advocates.

BET did not hold the same potential for fostering cozy or cooptive relationships as in DSS—for a basic organizational reason. BET's structure divided the work of the bureau into two major areas: on one side—policy, planning, and program development; on the other—operations management, The contract plans, programs, and awards were the responsibility of the first set of officials. Contract negotiations, monitoring, and technical assistance were carried out by the contract administrators in the operations management division. This meant that the bureaucrats with the most frequent, ongoing, and face-to-face contacts with contractors were not the same individuals who wrote the RFP's and decided awards for either of the titles. Personal relationships were therefore less likely to be a factor in choosing contractors and renewals. Certainly, contract administrators and contractors could have developed friendships that might have undermined the objectivity of the monitoring process and perhaps would have fed biased and inaccurate information into the awards process. This possibility did not occur, however, for at least four reasons: 1) the contract administrators and contractors had rather dissimilar educational and professional backgrounds, and were unlikely to develop these friendships; 2) program officials took a dominant role in the Title II awards, and did not rely on the administrators' feedback information; 3) the Title IV youth awards process was very objective and did not use performance information from the operations division; and 4) the three-year time limit on almost all contracts prevented loyalties from developing.

This explanation does not imply, however, that preferential treatment was nonexistant in BET's contracting. Both a planning official and some of the providers complained of cronyism between certain prime sponsors and the state DOL. The more vocal and sometimes more critical local agencies tended to receive more attention and assistance. Thus, certain public agencies were not only given more opportunities to compete for contracts, but also on occasion were given awards that, if they had been private agencies, they would not have received. Some of these decisions were made within the program offices, while others were made by the bureau and department directors.

Politics and Politicians in BET Contracting

In their evaluations, BET officials generally saw the activities of politicians in a more negative light than did DSS officials. One interviewee stated that they were too interfering, while the rest stated that they were only involved in contracts their constituents wanted. None said they were helpful, not involved enough, or hardly involved at all. The providers' experience with elected officials deviated from that of the bureaucrats, with two of the ten providers stating that politicians were generally helpful, three saying that they were hardly involved, and five claiming that they were only involved in contracts their constituents wanted.

The overall picture of politicians' involvement in state CETA contracts, however, is similar to that found in DSS' social services, even though political pressure was more often exerted by state legislators than by local officials. Politicians were interested in having funds channeled to their districts and sometimes to specific agencies as well. While they did not have many contacts with or influence over bureaucrats in their recommendations for awards, they were, on occasion, effective in changing the final choices of the bureau and department directors. As a result, BET had several sweetheart (or 'heaven above') contracts over the past years. An example of one was a Catholic agency (not included in my sample) that received both Title II and IV funds. Not only had the contract amounts exceeded the specified limit on youth contracts, but, according to a contract official, BET could have contracted with another agency to provide the services more effectively. A program head maintained, however, that usually politicians were not very successful at pushing poorly run programs.

Almost all of the officials expressed some resentment over the award changes made by DOL's appointed officials. A policy and planning supervisor said she would try "to make policy priorities that are good, but the decisions made at higher levels are not consistent with these." Another official explained that many "politicians may not have much information and understanding" of what BET was attempting to do with the CETA contracts—implying that if they did, they would not have pressured BET to alter their priorities. That analysis was probably too charitable. Even those who knew the goals of BET were not averse to tampering with the experts' recommendations. The department director had both a 'hand on' style of management where contracting out was concerned and some political ambitions of his own, which in combination meant that some capriciousness in funding was almost inevitable. Some of the award decisions probably derived from his use of contracts to achieve his own goals while others resulted from politicians who understood his style and political vulnerability. As with the DSS case, sweetheart contracts came from both elected officials or appointed department heads—both groups that tried to augment their political support by this means. Consequently, despite professional expertise and a model contracting process, the final choices were not always consistent with CETA regulations and the stated goal of maximizing service performance and effectiveness.

Conclusion

One of the intriguing questions in this type of research is: Why have officials chosen to contract out for services instead of using traditional bureaucratic methods of supply? For the DSS and DOL cases, the answer has both pragmatic and policy components. Decision makers were not persuaded by sophisticated cost-benefit studies or public choice arguments. Rather, federal policies encouraged service purchasing and state situations often made it attractive, if not necessary. In DSS, contracting out was originally seen as a method for increasing federal funding for social services through the seventy-five percent federal match. Since then, tradition, political pressures, and specialized services in the private sector ensured that the purchase-of-service approach would continue, especially since many local providers contributed the local donation for the state match. For BET, contracting out was used in part because the state-level department lacked the necessary expertise or agencies for the various programs they required. Purchasing services also gave them flexibility in service decisions and corresponded with the bureau's policy of granting contracts for innovative and experimental projects that in time would be locally supported.

In other respects as well, the rational decision-making process envisioned by public choice analysts has not been realized in human service contracting. Yet the two cases did not produce identical results. In part because of different historical and programmatic commitments, the two other areas of contracting decisions stand in clear contrast to one another. In DSS, thorough and objective needs assessments have been infrequent. Most attempts at assessing current needs and service supply have been perfunctory and heavily dependent upon provider input. The interests and needs of the inarticulate, unorganized clients and taxpayers have seldom been directly represented, despite Title XX intentions. This problem is not unique to Michigan's implementation of Title XX either. An Urban Institute study found that generally the states failed to produce comprehensive, systematic, and representative planning processes in social services.[7]

Even when available, needs information infrequently served as the major determinant in setting social service priorities and awarding contracts. Previous commitments to services and providers have often not allowed officials the flexibility to change their priorities, services, and contractors without political repercussions. DSS' early policy of granting contracts to almost any available contractors willing to make the donation set a pattern that was difficult to break, even when cutbacks and changes were necessary. Consequently, renewing contracts repeatedly has been the standard practice at the state level and in most counties. When making new contracts, decision makers usually preferred the experienced, reputable agencies that offered necessary services for DSS clients, with little regard for the cost and efficiency of the service delivery.

The decision-making process in state CETA contracts offers an interesting and necessary contrast to DSS' procedures. In particular, BET used systematic needs assessment methods that depended upon information from a variety of sources, not just vested interests. They were aimed at including both the relative needs of various target populations and the existing service supply through CETA programs. Decision makers have apparently used these means to set priorities, especially in the youth grant RFP. Perhaps the difference between the DSS and the BET systems was largely because CETA not only required that the information be gathered (as Title XX did), it also provided funds that were clearly earmarked for this purpose (as Title XX did not).

From the needs assessments to the proposal evaluations, the Title IV RFP process was designed to be a model of the rational, comprehensive approach to decision making. In large part, this process can be attributed to the availability of CETA funds to support this expensive process and the commitment of the program and policy supervisors to improving decisions. It is clear that not all bureaucrats were only interested in pushing contracts through as quickly as possible; they had some interest in finding better ways to accomplish their bureau's aims. Yet the results of the process were not all what BET officials had hoped for, since many of the proposals were unresponsive to their needs and the contractors' performance was inadequate. Part of this failure was due to the absence of the competition condition in the service environment. Moreover, BET's decision not to build its own service delivery system meant that it could not act as a backup when only undesirable alternatives were available.

In contrast, the Title II process was more similar to DSS', with a less structured, objective approach to considering proposals. But the imposition of a three-year limit on funds did mean that, except for a few cases, BET was not pressured into renewing contracts that no longer served its purposes.

Just as DSS and BET did not use contracting for cost reasons, neither did they choose among the small number of proposers on the basis of comparative costs of services. Generally, officials were interested in purchasing specialized services for clients—often ones that could not be directly compared. In DSS, agency reputation and experience were the major criteria for awards (where they had a real choice), while in BET, the proposal's design and responsiveness to the bureau's specifications were more critical.

In both DSS and BET, traditional standards of objectivity and fairness were not uniformly maintained in the decision-making process, due to favoritism in certain awards. In DSS, certain county contract coordinators preferred some contractors over others. In BET, public agencies were favored in solicitations and awards.

Elected and appointed officials were involved in making sweetheart contracts in both cases.

Although not entirely applicable to these cases, the alternative perspectives help to explain why officials would use contracting out to provide services. The organizational decision-making perspective predicted that governments would respond to artificial, organizational incentives to purchase—i.e., the federal match and the donation in DSS; the lack of BET capacity to produce its own services. The cooptation perspective expected that contractors, bureaucrats, and politicians would see the opportunities to build mutually beneficial relationships—though this reason may not have been of primary importance in either department.

Both the market imperfections and cooptation perspectives stress that suppliers will try to be involved in determining needs and services, to reduce competition and ensure renewals. Both the market imperfections perspective and the organizational decision making perspective emphasize that agencies often lack the requisite resources (time, expertise, money, and cognitive abilities) to obtain and assimilate information to make the best choices. Especially DSS' needs assessment and planning process was characterized by more input and information from current providers than from other competitors of clients. In general, poor clients do not have the resources or the opportunities to participate. In addition, DSS has had insufficient information to systematically analyze and compare the current demand *and* supply of the wide range of social services for various needy populations. Both the resources and commitment to improve needs assessments has been lacking, according to interviewees.

Where awards decisions were concerned, DSS and BET had to rely primarily on information about expected service costs, components, and performance from the service 'sellers,' who have both the incentives and opportunities to put their programs in the best light. For various reasons, BET officials failed to avail themselves of essentially free information about compliance and performance from the contract specialists in the operations division, to be used in determining awards. This problem was due to organizational barriers to communication—program staff and contract administrators were assigned different tasks and had different expertise. According to the contract specialists, this failure to obtain their evaluations and suggestions reflected the program and planning division's unwillingness to rely on the lower-status, less professional unit for program input. Yet the operations management division believed it had useful information with which to judge future success because of its role in writing and monitoring contracts.

Another area in which organizational realities constrained contracting choices was in the case of BET's youth contracts. Despite its ambitious efforts in needs assessments, solicitations, and award procedures, the bureaucratic requirement to spend all appropriated funds meant that some unresponsive and unreliable agencies received contracts.

Finally, according to the cooptation perspective, favoritism in awards, as well as in solicitations and needs assessments, should come as no surprise to those who understand political realities. Because of the need to build political support by bureaucrats, politicians, and contractors, certain agencies were disadvantaged, clients' needs were overlooked, and the purchased services may have been ineffective in reducing dependency.

6

The Watchdog Role

Now our attention focuses on one of the most important parts of the contract process—the government's monitoring and evaluation of cost and performance. Those in the public choice school who advocate contracting out as a solution to government inefficiency assume that the relevant government unit can determine that its money is spent as agreed upon, and that the performance and effectiveness of the services make the contracts worthwhile. Ideally, the contractor should undergo rigorous scrutiny in three areas—expenditures, compliance with the contract's specifications, and the long-range effectiveness of the services. The last type of evaluation is particularly necessary in the area of human services, since the goals are usually to change people, their behavior, and/or their circumstances. Obviously, the oversight role of governments also requires the utilization of these reviews—such that the cost and performance feedback has a direct effect upon future decisions. The contract owner can use this information to determine if the contract should be renewed, if another service agent should be sought, if the government should supply the service itself instead, or if the service needs to be provided at all. It is only with these options available that the government can act as an effective watchdog over the public purse and client services.

As in the previous chapters, we will examine whether this watchdog condition of contracting out is present, first, in the social services case, and then in the employment and training services in Michigan. The three alternative theoretical perspectives argue that primarily because of high information costs and bureaucratic self-interest, reviews will be infrequent and ineffective in monitoring expenditures and performance.

Review Procedures in DSS

In Michigan, the two most important parts of the DSS review process were the monitoring of expenditures (in accordance with DSS accounting methods) and the determination of eligibility for service recipients. The DSS' reviews were not generally oriented toward evaluating service performance or the effect of services on client dependency. Some variation existed among counties, however, since each county DSS determined the reviews it wished to perform. Only the periodic reporting of expenditures and units of service was required of providers by state contract administration.

The state contract management office was responsible for overseeing the expenditure and eligibility review processes and assisting counties and providers with the many forms. Contract specialists were to: 1) determine in a general way if adequate bookkeeping systems were in place; 2) review the providers' quarterly progress reports on enrollments and services performed; and 3) conduct on-site field visits to give assistance where problems existed, examine the facilities and services for compliance, and to go through files to check at random on client eligibility. Due to staff cuts, since FY 1978, the field visits were reduced in number and limited only to a few agencies or counties with obvious problems. The office was, therefore, almost exclusively concerned with examining contract compliance, not with service performance, quality, or impact.

If any performance reviews or in depth evaluations were done, they were conducted by the county DSS, often at the request of the county director or the Board of Social Services. County contract coordinators sometimes performed their own on-site visits as well. Because of inadequate staff and funding in most counties, however, these reviews were informal and infrequent. Only three of the seven counties reported doing more in depth forms of evaluation since Title XX was enacted, and then only for a few services. Clients were not contacted for their veiwpoints and suggestions, except by some providers in their own evaluation reports. Subcontractors were not required to be reviewed for their use of funds or for performance, since the main contractors were held responsible for their services. The information used for performance reviews was mainly compiled by the contractors themselves. Contractors wrote their own expenditure and progress reports and sent them to the county office. In short, the contractors could usually get by with filling out the required forms, since state and county scrutiny was spotty and depended so heavily on self-reporting.

The postaudit of expenditures was also used to check on costs and compliance. Some of the contractor agencies subcontracted with an independent accounting firm for an annual audit, included its cost in its contract budget, and sent copies of the report to the county and/or state offices. The internal audit staff of the state DSS also conducted audits of a random selection of agencies, or in response to a request by program or contract officials for suspicion of fraud, inadequate bookkeeping procedures, or noncompliance with the terms of the contract. Since they usually took place within six months to a year after the end of the contract, these fiscal audits' results were usually not known until the contracts were renewed once or even twice. Even though future contracts could not be made after negative findings, funds may have been misspent for a period of two or more years. One respondent reported that officials did not always prosecute even in clear cases of fraud because of political pressure. Instances of mismanagement of funds posed difficulties in recouping losses because of the expense involved and the contractors' apparent good intentions.

A few contracts were, however, revoked or terminated before the specified end of the contract year, for various reasons, including the improper use of funds, unsatisfactory service performance, failure to provide the specified service, or fouled-up bookkeeping procedures. Some of these contracts were ended by mutual agreement, as in cases where the provider was unable to get the program started up on time, while other contractors were only discovered to be in noncompliance when an audit was performed (e.g., a case where it was found that an agency did not exist). In addition, in FY 1980, several contracts were terminated and many reduced in funding because of the state's fiscal crisis, though the donated funds contracts were not as affected as the straight purchase contracts. Official suspensions or debarrments resulting from various cases of contractor fraud were not generally used, although a couple lawsuits were in the courts to recoup lost funds, and several contractors were unofficially eliminated for solicitations or awards because of previous experiences.

Opinions about DSS Reviews

Two questions about the review procedures in contracted services were asked of all the respondents to assist in evaluating the extent and effectiveness of DSS' watchdog role. One question offered a forced choice:

> In your area, do you believe that the monitoring and evaluation of contractors is:
> 1. too strict, with too much unnecessary and burdensome paperwork
> 2. not adequate to oversee expenditures
> 3. not adequate to evaluate performance
> 4. not strict enough to oversee expenditures *or* to evaluate performance adequately
> 5. just about right
> 6. some other response(s)?

None of the bureaucrats chose either of the first two alternatives. All of the state officials said the current review process was either inadequate to evaluate performance (two of six respondents), or inadequate for reviewing both expenditures and performance (four respondents). None of them said that the reviews were just about right. The seven county coordinators and service heads were more divided in their answers. Two of them (both of which had evidenced more cooptative tendencies) said they believed the monitoring and evaluations were just about right in their counties, although one of them admitted that performance reviews were just barely adequate. Three did not think efforts were sufficient for reviewing either costs or performance, while one said that performance was not evaluated adequately.

Although they agreed with some of the officials, the ten providers' opinions were more scattered across the responses. Unlike the state and county respondents, three contractors chose the first response, but they emphasized the unnecessary and burdensome paperwork more than the fact that the process was too strict. The part of their work that was heavily scrutinized was client eligibility, not their performance. Another three said the performance evaluations were inadequate, while two providers stated that both the expenditure and performance reviews were insufficient. Of the ten, two judged the process to be about right, although they also had some problems with it, as they revealed in their answers to the next question. One said the reviews were "O.K., but accountability is important, and monitoring can be improved." Most of the providers agreed in some way with the statement of a county services head that the review process was "terribly cumbersome from start to finish, and confusing for providers."

The following open-ended question was also asked of all respondents:

> What do you believe are the *major* problems involved in the monitoring and evaluation of performance?

Respondents pinpointed several problems, but the consensus was that DSS officials did not have the requisite resources of time, staff, money, and expertise to do careful reviews, so they hardly did them at all. They usually depended upon the providers to summarize their service quality and effectiveness in an annual report. State or county reviews were primarily a paper process, not evaluations of performance. Because service sites were physically removed from them and program supervisors, responsible county officials were unable to keep in frequent contact with providers and their staffs to monitor their performance on an ongoing basis, as was done with DSS caseworkers. Providers explained that little monitoring and evaluation was done by anyone, although some suggested it would have been healthy to have greater DSS scrutiny, involvement, and communication about their services during the contract year.

Almost all of the respondents reported having difficulty with various elements of the evaluation enterprise, and suggested that these were primary reasons for inadequate performance reviews. One of the major stumbling blocks was the inability to develop "a statistical evaluation tool that has both credibility and validity," in the words of a county coordinator. He and others emphasized that the social services literature on this subject was inadequate for their needs. Interviewees also mentioned the lack of standard evaluation measures of service quality, performance, outcomes, and impact. With many different services being purchased, this problem becomes more serious, since the same evaluation tool is inappropriate for all programs. Two officials stated it was also difficult to compare different agencies' performance and outcomes as a basis for award decisions because of sole source contracting—"it's like comparing apples and oranges," according to one respondent. A state program head reported that when her office attempted to develop some outcome measures for contracted services, the Michigan attorney general's office notified her that contractors could not be held legally accountable to meeting performance outcomes; they could only be held responsible for performing the service as agreed upon in the contract.

Several respondents also mentioned that, ideally, frequent client evaluations and follow-ups should be done as a method of measuring the contractors' performance and effectiveness. Although some providers tried to obtain the views of their clients, systematic studies were often impractical because of fluid populations and a lack of knowledge of "how to develop a workable and honest client evaluation."

DSS' procedures and organizational structure were also blamed for the inadequacies of performance reviews. According to county officials and providers, the state did not provide consistent policies and specific guidelines about how, when, and why reviews were to be conducted. A state program official said that it was the counties' responsibility to develop review and reporting systems to give them the necessary information, but they had failed to do it. A contract management section respondent summarized this major problem as "deciding who is suposed to do the job in this bureaucratic mess." This critical oversight activity appeared to fall between the jurisdictions of various units and was viewed as an undesirable task by everyone.

From their vantage point, providers saw some additional problems in the procedures that were employed. One of the few review methods consistently used by state monitors was to visit an agency, usually on an annual basis, with the sole purpose of pulling one or two cases out of the files to examine them for eligibility, compliance, and completeness. Some thought this method was both inadequate and unfair. One provider also complained about the lack of monitoring consistency, in that "different monitors looked for different things," meaning providers were uncertain of how to comply with DSS reviews. Adding to the problem, according to respondents, was that DSS reviewers often knew little about the services that agencies delivered or about the clients' needs. This ignorance affected not only the methods and measures used to monitor and evaluate, but also the needs assessments and proposal reviews.

BET's Review Procedures

BET's goals for the Governors' Grants were improved coordination, experimentation, and effectiveness. Given these aims, thorough and objective reviews were critical in two areas—contract compliance and program effectiveness. By these methods the government could be assured that clients were receiving the kinds and quality of services they required. And BET could gain useful knowledge about the cause and effect relationships that operate under different projects.

Most of the Title II and IV contracts were reviewed indirectly by the bureau, however, through contractors' self-reporting of expenditures and progress in accordance with BET's guidelines and forms. All contract monitoring was performed by contract administrators, but they mainly checked the providers' performance and expenditure forms for simple compliance with the terms of the contract (e.g., correct number of enrollees, overspending and underspending). As with DSS contracts, the most rigorous scrutiny was reserved for determining participants' eligibility. A lottery system was used for selecting clients' files to verify information. Unlike the DSS reviews, however, the monitoring of expenditures did not appear to be particularly thorough during the life of the contract. Even when the provider was found to be in noncompliance, the contract could not be terminated if the provider showed good faith. Contract administrators provided technical assistance to move the program or administration in the agreed-upon direction.

On-site field visits were first employed for the early part of FY 1981, and then only infrequently. Thereafter, the personnel were no longer available to make visits because of staff cuts and travel curtailments. (BET had plenty of federal funds for contracts and staff salaries, but it suffered along with other departments in the state's personnel reduction efforts.) On rare occasions, contract monitors had called on subcontractors, but most of the subcontracted services were only indirectly reviewed through the contractors' reports. Title II coordination and linkage contracts appeared to receive even less review, since they did not serve client populations directly.

Only infrequently did BET's program development division produce in depth evaluations to determine if certain programs were effective, whether changes were necessary, and if they should be continued. Several of the provider respondents suggested that BET did not seem to be particularly interested in their results—even when some had not performed very well in meeting their objectives. This failure to conduct performance reviews was obviously inconsistent with BET's avowed purpose to fund model programs. How else was BET to determine it was using its funds wisely?

Some of the providers compiled final reports on their projects, through their own initiative. These ranged from very professional, objective, and thorough analyses to brief summaries of the program, completion rates, placements, etc. Sometimes contractors included participant evaluations and follow-up surveys; these were the only means BET had of obtaining client viewpoints, apart from a participants' grievance procedure. It was unclear, however, what, if anything, BET did with these reports. It did not disseminate information about the model or demonstration projects that were successful in meeting employment needs, yet that would have been a natural fulfillment of their goals.

The postaudit was by far the most thorough means of verifying expenditures and contract compliance for the BET contracts. All contracts of $100,000 and over were routinely audited by private firms, while each year ten percent of all other contracts were randomly selected for audits by the regional office of the federal DOL. Since only a few contracts were made for over the $100,000 level, many of the contracts actually did not receive a thorough review. As in DSS, audits were performed some time after the end of the contract year; if expenditure and compliance monitoring had not spotted any irregularities, the problems could go undiscovered for almost two years.

Of the Title II and IV contracts, approximately five were terminated for noncompliance with the contract and/or CETA regulations in the three years I studied. Several other agencies voluntarily terminated their contracts before the specified end of the contract, for a variety of reasons, including late start-ups, staff problems, etc. One additional contract was revoked when BET learned that the agency director was in jail. Because of these and other experiences with certain public and private agencies, BET decided several agencies would not be considered for future awards.

Opinions about BET Reviews

Interviewees were also questioned whether they believed the monitoring and evaluation of contractors was:

1. too strict, with too much unnecessary and burdensome paperwork
2. not adequate to oversee expenditures
3. not adequate to evaluate performance
4. not strict enough to oversee expenditures *or* to evaluate performance adequately
5. just about right
6. some other response(s)?

BET officials were very critical of their own review methods. Four of the five who answered the question gave the fourth response — the procedures were not adequate for expenditures or for performance. Of the contractors, four of the ten said that the procedures were just about right, but the other respondents were more critical. Two who chose "some other response" combined two of the alternatives — the monitoring and evaluating required too much burdensome paperwork *and* was inadequate to evaluate performance. The respondent who gave the first choice answered in the same vein by saying the reviews were not too strict; they just required too much time-consuming paperwork.

When they were asked to specify the major problems associated with the reviews, there was almost unanimity among BET officials. All but one of them answered that they had insufficient time, staff, and travel funds necessary to do the critical task of on-site field monitoring. Consequently, officials were unable to assist contractors as effectively as they might have, nor could they determine what the providers' administration and program staff were actually doing. The following problems were also given by officials: "contract work statements are written so we cannot hold them to it"; some resistance by contractors to reviews, since they were somewhat protective of their records; and it was "difficult to develop tools and measures for evaluation," partly because of the different goals and priorities held by providers and various state officials.

Two familiar themes ran through the responses of the providers: the paperwork load was heavy and the performance reviews were inadequate. A constant vexation were the various forms that were required by CETA and BET. For the same program, some contractors were required to fill out quite different sets of forms for each funding source, even though the information was essentially the same. Some of the contractors said that they had fallen behind schedule in submitting reports on verifying eligibility because of the unrealistic paperwork and time frames. A provider claimed that even with the monitoring and the expenditure, eligibility, and progress reports, a dishonest contractor could still find methods of successfully defrauding the government.

Complaints about BET's narrow view of performance were raised by several providers. They noted that although BET officials talked about achieving good results, BET focused most of its efforts on forms and eligibility—not on performance outcomes, service quality, and client follow-ups. BET's single measure of success was whether or not a program participant had been placed in employment immediately after completion of a program. One of the contractors found this emphasis on placement numbers to be quite inadequate for his program for adjudicated minority high school dropouts. Other long- and short-term positive by-products of the program were also significant accomplishments for enrollees—e.g., staying out of trouble or going back to school. Another interviewee with a linkage contract stated that her agency had no external source of evaluation for essential feedback about their training programs. She suggested that "internal evaluations are always slanted" in agencies' own favor, such that the results would not usually be reliable and valid.

Conclusion

Although their criticisms were fewer in number and narrower in scope, BET officials and contractors seemed to have the same problems as DSS respondents did in the monitoring and evaluation of their programs: the paperwork; the inadequate evaluation measures and tools; the lack of time, staff, and funds. Both departments emphasized client eligibility verification, did less well on reviewing expenditures, and failed in evaluating all but a few programs for performance and effectiveness. Everyone agreed that not enough monitoring and evaluation was being done, and with the state's fiscal squeeze the situation was unlikely to change in the near future. The unfortunate irony of Michigan's fiscal squeeze was that while the necessity for closer scrutiny, better information, and complete evaluations increased, the resources available for them decreased.

Both the market imperfections perspective and the organizational decision-making perspective predicted that the costs associated with gathering useful information about contract performance would prohibit thorough monitoring and evaluation procedures. Thus, low cost or free information in the form of contractors' own reviews and the client eligibility checks required by Title XX and CETA became the primary methods for determining compliance and performance. The validity and reliability of these approaches to performance are obviously questionable.

The organizational perspective also focused on the various organizational difficulties involved in the government oversight role. Because of the fragmentation of contract authority, DSS clearly had difficulties determining who, if anyone, was responsible for performance reviews. Various sections of the state government and the counties had slices of responsibility for oversight activities, meaning that everyone pointed at other participants for their failure, and little was actually accomplished. In BET, due to strained relations between the two divisions responsible for contracts, those who monitored the ongoing contract operations and those who planned for services and programs failed to communicate in a cooperative manner about operational and performance problems. Providers received the message that BET was unconcerned about its performance and effectiveness. This inference by contractors was a dangerous one to foster, since CETA and BET's stated goals could be jeopardized. Even though it was unclear to what extent BET and DSS actually made awards decisions on the basis of performance and/or effectiveness, officials should have tried to maintain the impression, if not the reality, that these factors were critical to contractors' future funding.

7

The Costs and Benefits of Human Service Contracting Out

The main thrust of this book has been to examine the three conditions of contracting out (competition, rational decision making, and adequate reviews) implied by the public choice argument. We can go beyond this examination of the contracting process and look at the results of the process by evaluating whether the expectations of lower cost and better services were fulfilled in Title XX and the state CETA programs. The previous chapters indicated that in many areas, the ideal process of contracting out does not occur as some might expect or hope. It is possible that the outcomes do measure up to advocates' expectations, however, either because of some 'hidden hand' mechanism, or the presence of some identifiable compensating conditions. This exploration will help to put into perspective the various advantages and disadvantages some associate with contracting out as raised in the first chapter. Although contracting officials lacked hard data on these questions, most were willing to estimate the general outcomes and problems of contracting in their experience. Therefore, we will depend upon the opinions of the various participants in the process to evaluate cost and performance. Their views are interesting and enlightening, because they reflect attitudes and beliefs that probably affected their contract relationships and shaped contract decisions. Nonetheless, this discussion must be read with caution, since direct evidence on the outcomes is lacking.

The Costs and Quality of Purchased Social Services

According to contracting advocates, the strongest argument in favor of purchasing services is that it will lead to significant cost savings for government. However, as we have seen, the social services profession has been more concerned with meeting clients' various needs through contracting out. Thus, it is important to examine whether costs have been reduced anyway—perhaps due to inherent economies of scale in private agencies, lower salary levels, more efficient use of resources, or other factors. To determine what respondents believed, I asked them this question:

> In the contracts and services you work with, do you think contracting with private agencies or firms costs less than, about the same as, or more than, government delivery of those services would?

In response, the state and county officials were uncertain about the relative costs, since no one had made such comparisons. However, when pressed, seven of the thirteen public officials said that costs were lower than public delivery would be, and, not surprisingly, eight of the ten providers agreed. Of the bureaucrats, five out of seven county officials believed that the costs were lower under contracts, while only two of the six state officials concurred (thirty-three percent).

Some of the officials emphasized the difficulty in accurately assessing all of the costs, since the contract amount is no indication of the total cost of administration and service. The reason they and providers gave for why contracted services might be less expensive came down to one major factor—salaries and fringe benefits for workers in private counseling agencies were usually lower than for county DSS caseworkers.[1] One official added that the twenty-five percent donation obviously made it less expensive to contract out. Another said that the government benefits by using outside providers that have already established an organization of specialized personnel.

On the other hand, several officials argued that although it seems less costly to contract out, several factors cancel out the apparent savings on some of the salaries and fringe benefits, and may make the service more expensive in the long run: the extra, sometimes hidden, costs of contracting paperwork, administration, and review; greater expenses for some of the more specialized services for which pay scales were significantly higher; the opinion that 'there are as many rip-off artists in the private sector as in the public'; and the belief that per-unit cost of services are lower in the public sector, primarily because of the larger case loads of DSS caseworkers.

Even if the cost of DSS contracted services were equal to or less than publicly provided services, efficiency and effectiveness may not characterize the services if the performance was unacceptable. Therefore, the respondents were given this question:

> For the contracts and services you work with, do you think contracting with private agencies or firms results in poorer service, about the same quality of service, or better service for recipients than government service delivery would?

With this question, an interesting phenomenon occurred. While nine out of the ten providers judged the quality of their services to be better than the government's, this time, county contracts coordinators disagreed. Instead, the majority (five out of seven) said the quality was only equal to that of services delivered by the county DSS. This result may be due to a closer observation of DSS caseworkers and contractors, or because of a possible county/public sector loyalty. But on this question, half of the six state bureaucrats claimed that the services were better in the private sector. For the totals, ninety-one percent (twenty-one respondents) stated that private social service delivery was equal to or better than public service delivery. No one said that contracted services were poorer in quality. (Yet it must be remembered that some of these individuals had been chosen at least in part because of their sympathy with private organizations and often saw themselves as advocates of contracting out in the system.)

Respondents were generally less tentative in their answers and comments on this matter. Although again they had no hard data comparing the contractors' performance with that of DSS, many respondents were definite in their answers because of personal experiences, social work studies, and/or their application of logic to the issue. Public officials who said that the private services were generally better gave the following reasons: "they don't have to serve DSS clients, so they don't burn out or get discouraged"; "generally, the education and experience level of private staff is higher" (e.g., a higher number of M.A. degrees); "reimbursement is based on quality and outcomes, not existance—we can terminate the contract otherwise"; "more flexibility to drop the contract"; "we buy it with the expectation that the service will be better than can be done in-house"; "better oversight"; "personalized, smaller case loads, greater variety of services, identification with clients is closer, and they can select their clients" (those besides the state recipients).

Several respondents, however, qualified their statements about the quality being equal to or better in the contracted services with comments like these: services are better if it is a "specialized agency that does things the government doesn't," but about the same quality if the service is counseling; if the service is already provided in the community, it is better, but if it is an unpopular service, then the government could provide better service (e.g., protective services for children); "it depends on the agency—some are better than others." A services supervisor in a medium-sized county mentioned that a recent comparison of children's foster services showed that the private agencies were lagging behind DSS' resolution of cases, such that the county was considering eliminating private supply. Those who claimed that service quality was roughly equal in the two sectors said this resulted because of: equal oversight; the fact that government has the money to keep an agency going, "high standards in both the agencies and DSS"; "accountability is about equal"; they "must see to it, through monitoring"; "they're all skilled professionals, whether in the government or not."

Agency directors and representatives were even more enthusiastic about the private services, but they gave different reasons: "specialization and a smaller span of control over quality"; "better attitudes toward work and service, as well as better knowledge of how to help clients"; "DSS caseworkers have heavier caseloads, but we have more time and personal contact"; "staff turnover is much lower"; "better staff selection and supervision"; "more participation in running program"; "smaller units"; "greater motivation, creativity, and professionalism."

Other Benefits of DSS Contracting

Contracting proponents have not only expected that cost savings with good quality services could be realized, but they have also maintained that contracting would be likely to lead to a slowdown in the growth of government which is an important goal for most public choice thinkers. But has this been a result of the DSS experience?

Government growth can be examined from two perspectives — growth in the expenditures of government, and growth in the number of public employees. In both respects, the DSS contracting experience does not meet up with public choice expectations. The original federal legislation was designed to *spend* money and because of the way the law and regulations were worded, at uncontrollable rates, until 1972. Michigan's share of the federal grants grew from approximately $16 million in FY 1971 to over $100 million in FY 1976, in part because of the increase in purchase of services through both agreements and contracts.[2] Contracts started off slowly and never reached the levels of some other states; yet they were a way of increasing the federal participation more rapidly than possible with direct services, and they have continued to be an important means for providing services.[3] Where government had previously not funded services, by the mid-seventies, the state had given out large amounts of federal money by contract, and by doing so, became committed to continuing many of these, in part because of the dependency of both clients and providers.

An argument can be made that at least the costs to the *state* government did not increase significantly under Title XX contracting out, due to the federal participation and the donated funds. However, both before and after decentralization, as DSS became more concerned with programmatic integrity, accountability, and the imposed Title XX matching ceiling, large numbers of people were hired by DSS to make and administer the contracts. Consequently, not only did more federal monies get spent on contracts, but also additional state funds were necessary for contract administration, not all of which was covered by Title XX. Nonetheless, it is true that the state DSS was not spending relatively large sums for these services, and its behavior might have been different if the money had not been so readily available and if the funds had been appropriated by the state legislature.

While curtailing government was not a realized benefit in this case, DSS respondents did suggest a somewhat unexpected benefit of contracting out for DSS services in response to a rather vague question:[4]

> Do you believe that using private contractors to produce and deliver public services is somehow more democratic or less democratic than using public employees?
> 1. more democratic
> 2. less democratic
> 3. doesn't have anything to do with democratic ideals
> Why?

Respondents may have had a fairly hazy notion of the meaning of 'democratic' and nine of the twenty-three did not see any connection; yet twelve participants suggested some interesting reasons for why they believed that contracting out was more democratic than in-house service supply. The most frequent reply by officials and providers was that outside agencies offered clients a choice—i.e., they could either use the county DSS caseworkers, or be referred to a private agency for usually more specialized assistance. So if democratic connoted freedom, this was viewed as an important advantage over in-house services. Three respondents gave answers that referred to the notion that contracting out involves more people in the decision-making and service process, and thus, according to a provider, related to our democratic system being "based on pluralism." Other reasons for choosing 'more democratic' were: "doesn't expand government," "better services," "more resources for community problems," "private agencies are more accountable and responsive." The two interviewees who thought contracting out was less democratic saw political favoritism as a problem. Thus, while some responses were directly related to the general advantages and disadvantages of contracting out, several saw the relevance of contracting to broader theories of public choice and pluralism.

I also asked providers about the major advantages they realized with receiving DSS contracts. Their replies can be categorized into four major areas: 1) the funds allowed them to continue operating with some certainty at least for another year; 2) they were able to provide a necessary service for clients; 3) they were able to expand their programs; and 4) the contracts sometimes put agencies in a better position for private funds. A family counseling director said that the DSS contracts, for as long as he received them, gave his agency money for a service that it had already been providing voluntarily on a smaller scale.

Perceived Problems of the Purchasing Process

Although they realized several obvious advantages, the providers also perceived some major problems with receiving contracts. Two answers were often given: 1) excessive paperwork ("too much attention to procedures, not enough on services"); and 2) late payments in recent years. The contractors also complained about various stages of the process—planning ("little advance notice about funds and contracts," "deadlines are too tight"); donations (with the money management agencies having trouble finding the twenty-five percent); award decisions ("arbitrary and capricious"); monitoring (see previous chapter); and service delivery ("underutilization" by DSS clients).

For their part, state and county officials saw several serious problems with DSS contracts with private agencies, some of which coincided with agencies' perceptions. They focused on both DSS' problems and agencies' inadequacies. One state program official mentioned the difficulty of taking away or reducing contracts, while another admitted that the state sometimes produced unrealistic program descriptions for outside suppliers. Since they worked on the budgets and proposals, the state contract managers complained about both payment delays and the inadequate fiscal record keeping by contractors. More critical than the state officials, the county bureaucrats said that DSS' problems were often operational and procedural, with inadequate time frames, high administrative costs, and difficulty "translating DSS language into agency language." In one medium-sized county, the services director found an employment agency that was willing to do a small pilot study for DSS' hard-to-place clients, but because of the many state requirements, the agency gave up its pursuit of a contract. In effect, the process itself can act as an impediment to competition and choice.

DSS' decision-making process posed a major problem for some county respondents, since smaller counties had difficulty finding providers and donors due to the lack of competition; officials were uncertain of what to purchase; and the Board of Social Service made the final decision, but did not get involved in the day-to-day work. In one county, program staff relations with the providers were viewed as uncooperative. The problem with agencies, on the other hand, was that they did not give "enough consideration" to small contracts; some agencies did not have "good public relations programs to sell themselves"; not all agencies were "geared toward lower-class DSS clients"; they were often dependent on government funds, so it was difficult to cut funds; and they had difficulty understanding the forms and the process, so an extensive start-up period was usually required for new contracts.

When questioned about the major tensions in their work, state officials offered answers that reflected some basic organizational problems faced by public bureaucracies: communication gaps between the state program offices and contract management, lack of clarity about contract responsibilities, coordination problems, lack of acceptance of contract management section, too much paperwork, not enough time for planning and programming, no advance information about budgets; no long-term, five-year plan for social services (with the blame for the latter two problems being placed on the Congress and the state legislature). County contract coordinators also mentioned some of these problems, but added some different responses. They used similar terms to describe their often frustrating roles: "trouble shooter," "negotiator," "mediator," on the "hot seat," and "pulled in different directions" between the state, the contractors, the politicians, and the county staff. Their jobs had been made more demanding because of the recent cutbacks, and several complained of hostility, inadequate funding, and the difficulty in allocating scarce dollars.

The Costs and Quality of Purchased Employment Services

We have already noted several differences between DSS and BET contracting. We should also evaluate if BET's programs measure up to the positive expectations of reduced costs and better services. However, assessing the comparative costs and quality of in-house versus private service provision in Titles II and IV poses a problem for this study, since virtually all direct and coordination services were purchased by BET, either from public or private agencies. As a result, respondents had little empirical basis for comparing either the cost or the quality of services. Interviewees could, nonetheless, compare the relative costs and performance of private and public contractors. All of the BET officials had worked with both types of providers under the two titles. The public choice literature has maintained that either public or private agents can be used to achieve their efficiency goals, but recently some writers have argued that the private sector is inherently superior to public production.[5] Therefore, it is not inappropriate to examine the viewpoints of contracting actors concerning the two types of suppliers. When BET respondents were asked whether "contracting with private agencies costs less than, about the same as, or more than, government delivery of those services," they focused on the effects of using private versus public contractors, rather than the effect of contracting out itself. The answers of the state officials and the contractors differed markedly. While none of the BET officials said the costs of private agencies were less than government agencies, six of the ten provider respondents claimed they were. Three interviewees of each group believed costs were equal (half of the bureaucrats, thirty percent of the contractors); one from each group said costs were higher with private contractors; and two BET officials stated that relative costs depended more on the staff, the service, and the agency's experience than on whether it was public or private.

Respondents provided a variety of reasons for their answers. Those who believed private costs were generally equal to or greater than public production, commented: "private agencies underestimate how much it costs"; all contracts are cost reimbursement contracts with the same CETA guidelines; and there is "tremendous overhead" with some private agencies. On the other hand, those providers who claimed that the costs were lower with private agencies gave many of the same reasons as were given by the DSS respondents who compared private to in-house supply. In their view, the government contractor agencies incur more expenses because of bureaucracy, red tape, civil service, and higher salaries, while private agencies are more flexible and efficient, are forced to live within financial restraints, have less overhead and lower salaries, and are motivated by profit.

Interviewees were also questioned about the comparative quality of public versus private service provision, with the same three options. Again the state officials and the contractors disagreed in their answers. None of those from BET said that private agencies performed any better than public agencies. Four officials believed that the services were about equal; one contract administrator concluded from her experience that private agencies provided poorer services; another official said that the service quality depended upon the agencies' and staff members' level of experience.

A policy and planning official with experience in both the private and public sectors asserted that each type of agency had certain strengths and weaknesses for CETA contracting purposes—a comment that seemed to coincide with various statements made by both BET and DSS respondents. Because they had more experience in government programs and direct services, public agencies were usually better able to run programs, handle low-income clients, and meet BET's specific needs. Generally, nonprofit agencies had "a good programmatic sense," but their administrative skills were frequently inadequate. This official attributed this failing to the fact that many of these agencies "live hand-to-mouth because of their grant dependence." On the other hand, private, proprietary firms have better administrative skills, yet they were not usually very competent in providing the program and services to clients. The advantage of the private over the public agencies was that the private providers are "hungrier, so they want to cooperate." Another contract supervisor put it this way: "they are more likely to be responsive to corrective action" because of their greater need for funds.

As might be expected, seven of the ten contractors answered that private agency service quality was better than government's. The other three alternatives were chosen by one respondent each. Those who said the services were better in the private sector gave these familiar reasons: more flexibility, less bureaucracy, more personal contact, fewer regulations, greater expertise, better staff, less political interference. In addition, they claimed, at least in theory, if the agencies did not perform well, they would lose funding, giving them a strong incentive for good performance.

These responses and comments of the agency representatives are consistent with the answers given by DSS providers, as well as in keeping with the general thrust of many public choice scholars. It appears that those associated with private agencies believe that public agencies, whether under contract or not, are inferior in most cost and performance respects to private agencies. The contractors' opinion that private agencies have more incentives to maintain good services seems to be substantiated by the comments of some officials. But their overall performance would only be better if all other factors contributing to quality services were otherwise equal and that may not be the case for some agencies.

The question still remains, however: Have the expectations of cost reduction and improved services been realized by BET's heavy reliance on contracting out? Although there is no direct evidence on this matter in the interviews, certain factors can be considered to clarify this issue. Some large initial costs of building an agency or various programs were avoided by using existing specialized agencies. (Certainly the contracts helped to cover some overhead and administrative costs these agencies incurred, but it is probably less than the cost of starting from virtually nothing.) On the other hand, BET sustained significant administrative expenses directly and exclusively due to purchasing services from a wide range of different suppliers. The costs of contract administration appeared high, as the DSS administrators suggested. Not only did they negotiate and monitor the contracts, but the contract administrators also provided a great deal of technical assistance to providers — assistance that was especially necessary when new contractors were used. In a sense, then, BET absorbed program start-up costs each time a new agency was used, both in the cost of the contract for the agency's administrative needs and in the personnel costs for BET administrators.

The issue of comparative service quality is a difficult one. It is unclear whether private service quality is inherently better than public provision because of the structure of public and private agencies. If private services are usually better, then the positive answers of the DSS officials and providers can be explained in those terms — not just because of the contract mechanism. This would conform with the answers of DOL contractors as well. What is interesting in the DOL case, however, is that the BET officials saw few differences in service quality between the public and private agencies. This cannot be explained by loyalty to some public agencies, as we might conclude about the DSS county officials' failure to say that private services were better than the county's. In addition, officials were often dissatisfied with the performance of their contractors—both the public and private providers. The youth contracts, many of which were with private agencies, were particularly disappointing. The first year's enrollment and placement rates were low and several of the agencies even had difficulty gearing up their agencies for operation. This result indicates a problem with purchasing human services—contracting units must depend upon other agencies both to design their own programs and then to implement them. Contractors' efforts may not coincide with the goals of the officials; yet, in the BET case, these services were purchased nevertheless, because of the lack of alternatives. BET did not have its own in-house staff to provide more desirable services. Nor were there any other public or private agencies to solicit since all of them had already been invited to submit proposals. Consequently, the services were not of uniformly good quality, by both the officials' and providers' admissions. Reliance on outside agents means that the contracting unit can lose control over the services themselves. Therefore, contractors may not meet the government's objectives.

Benefits of BET Contracting Out

Just as it has been difficult to evaluate the expectations of lower cost and better services, determining if government growth has been slowed through BET contracting out is also problematic. Many factors affect both personnel and budget growth, and, we have no measures of what would have occurred if the services had not been purchased. It can be speculated that growth may have been held in check by the use of outside contractors. Contracting out and the usual three-year limit on funding may have prevented some ineffective programs from becoming institutionalized—as is apt to occur in bureaucracies.

Government growth, however, should not be analyzed only from the narrow view of BET's budget and personnel growth. BET made funds available to other state and local public agencies that found it necessary to add staff to accommodate an increased demand. In addition, when the BET funds were no longer forthcoming, local prime sponsors or city governments often contributed the funds necessary to keep projects going. After three years of service to a community, there may have been significant pressure to continue the larger projects — even if they were not particularly successful, or were not congruent with a local unit's priorities. Many local governments throughout the country have had difficulty withdrawing or refusing their support for programs that have been started with federal and state funds.

To learn of any additional dissimilarities between DSS and BET, the employment and labor interviewees were asked if they believed that contracting for services was more or less democratic than in-house supply. With one exception, the state respondents thought contracting out had nothing to do with democracy. The one who saw a connection said that she did not believe in big government, and thought private organizations should have a larger role in the services. The providers were split evenly between seeing no relevance to democracy and saying that purchasing services was more democratic. Compared to DSS, their answers did not stress the client's choice of service providers, since there was no choice involved. However, two respondents focused on the government's expanded choice and ability to pick the best agencies. Others emphasized the pluralism that contracting out introduces: "more participation and involvement by private organizations"; more citizen input; "supports private enterprise." One of the respondents saw that each of the two service approaches "lends itself to being influenced by different factions." Again, these interviewees had a vague idea of the meaning of democracy, but did associate contracting out with some broader political issues.

When questioned about the advantages of BET contracts, the provider respondents gave similar replies to those from DSS providers; 1) the contracts enabled them to deliver a needed service; 2) the funds were certain for one year, once approved; 3) BET gave them an opportunity to demonstrate their projects; and 4) the awards helped to increase their prestige with other government units. Comparing BET to other government agencies, providers stated that the bureau was flexible, fair, and cooperative; in one case, more flexible than the city of Detroit was for a youth program; and in another, less highly politicized than prime sponsors.

Perceived Problems of the BET Purchasing Process

BET contractors appeared to be more positive about their government relationship than the DSS contractors were (probably because their money had not been cut—yet). However, most of the BET contractors saw some problems, similar to those raised by DSS respondents. Many of their complaints focused on the detailed forms; restrictive CETA regulations (which BET complied with more rigorously than some); contract processing delays; late payments; and the lack of time, long-range planning, and multi-year contracts. Other answers included: "too often the contract and program is started before they raise technical problems"; not enough time to gear up a new program; difficulty in getting contracts; lack of consultation with BET and other providers; lack of participant referrals from the Department of Corrections (for a female ex-offender program); inadequate reviews.

When asked for their major problems with contracting out, BET officials repeated some themes woven throughout this book and chapter. The planning and program officials focused primarily on the front end of the contracting process, with problems in CETA regulations and lack of choice: "participant services are complex to purchase because of the regulations that protect clients" and were designed to eliminate previous abuses; the "need to translate everything" for the agencies; regulations' attention to procedures, so the "program gets lost in the process"; political awards; poor proposals and poor implementation; the need to award contracts to undeserving agencies, because no other agencies were available. For their part, the contract administrators mentioned several difficulties in the implementation stage, especially that the various agencies had different procedures and goals, and often had equally confusing bureaucracies. Thus, the administrators had to muddle through several sets of bureaucracies, red tape, and contact people. In addition, they stressed that agencies had inadequate time to "get a working knowledge of our regulations and goals."

BET officials also emphasized that, as in DSS, organizational conflicts and the lack of time produced the major tensions in their work. Because of late congressional and federal decisions, they found it difficult to compose good programs. A contract administrator saw her valuable time consumed by "going through levels, different people, priorities, and programs," which added to the general delay between receiving poposals and signing the contracts. With responsibility for the contracting process and decisions divided among various actors, a supervisor complained about the political decisions and capriciousness; the operations division employees expressed their frustration with the program and planning division, which "doesn't recognize our professionalism"; and another respondent stated that the questions about contracting responsibilities and policy interpretation increased her tension.

Conclusion

Does the absence of a rational decision-making process, of competition, and of an adequate watchdog role mean that DSS, BET, and their clients did not receive low cost, good quality services? Not necessarily. Our limited exploration of the expected benefits of contracting out indicates that at least DSS' privately provided services were generally rated as of good quality—at least equal to county service supply—even though BET's were seen as less than successful, for various reasons. DSS was able to augment its programs by using more specialized and expert outside agencies (e.g., money management agencies, rehabilitation agencies, agencies geared toward certain racial groups). The strong professional ethic, the expertise, and the commitment to the needy help to explain why most of the DSS providers and certainly some of the BET agencies performed well under contract. Agency representatives were proud of their agencies and their accomplishments. It probably can be safely said that at least some agencies worked at providing their services at acceptable cost levels because their costs were scrutinized—particularly in recent years.

I am not convinced, however, that significant cost reductions were realized in either the DSS or BET cases, considering the high administrative costs. Any savings to the state (as compared with in-house provision) have occurred because of the donation requirement, the BET match, and the federal source of the funds, which are intergovernmental and policy factors aimed at attaining other goals in the services. The legislation and the availability of outside providers contributed to the growth, not the curtailment of government in the DSS case. And where government did not grow, the private agencies did—and became more dependent upon government funding. What the BET case illustrated was that during severe fiscal stress, the state government realized personnel and travel cuts in the bureau, but because of the federal source of CETA, expanded its contracting with outside agencies, only without the staff for oversight of the contracts. While these outcomes do not necessarily indict contracting per se, they illustrate how this method of service supply can be used for quite different purposes and leads to different outcomes than those envisioned by contracting advocates.

These tentative conclusions about contracting results do not quite correspond with any of the four theoretical perspectives. While the public choice argument expected reduced costs and improved services, the three others predicted poorer services, perhaps even higher costs, and an expansion of government expenditures. Some of the three alternative perspectives' ideas were realized in the contracting process, but not completely in the results. The lack of experience in certain areas, the poor state of the Michigan economy, and the organizational necessity of spending all allocations partially explain why several of the BET projects, even by the agencies' own admission, were failures. But the agencies' professionalism and commitment provide strong reasons for the success of other projects. The contract mechanism itself or the three conditions that we expected to make it work may not have been the only factors producing the outcomes. Yet in the complete absence of other service alternatives, fairness in decisions, and review procedures, would the results be the same? Perhaps not. There may be some threshold level under which more contractors would take advantage of the system.

8

Concluding Analysis of Conditions and Perspectives of Contracting Out

This book has tried to unite two types of analysis: 1) the development of the economic, political, and organizational perspectives that pertain to the public choice prescription for contracting out, and 2) an empirical examination of human services contracting within two departments of Michigan state government in terms of the three conditions of contracting. This study offers a unique inquiry into this timely subject: it has taught us much about the actual process involved in contracting for services in Michigan under two major federal acts; it suggests ways in which the public choice model of contracting out is inadequate for understanding the implementation realities of DSS and DOL contracting; and the relevance of the three alternative social science traditions has been affirmed in several important respects.

This concluding chapter will highlight the major findings from the two departments in an effort to determine why the three major conditions were largely absent in the contracting process. Because of inadequacies in the public choice approach, the applicability of the three alternative perspectives for explaining contracting out will also be reviewed. From this, we can begin the task of identifying suitable conditions for successful contracting out, and consider alternative approaches to human services delivery. We will conclude by addressing some unresolved issues that bear further consideration and study.

Comparison of DSS and BET Contracting

An obvious starting point for reviewing human services contracting is to compare the goals of the contracting advocates with those of the federal legislation affecting social services and CETA programs. The social services grants were designed to increase the number of clients and the kinds of social services available to the needy. In BET, the CETA titles were aimed at coordinating employment and training services and promoting model projects. In both cases, cutting costs or improving efficiency were not major aims. Thus, the contracting systems and decisions were not made to maximize the objectives of most contracting supporters. Is it unfair then to measure the procedures and outcomes according to the yardstick of competition and reduced cost? Not at all, since some would believe that significant savings would result simply from using outside suppliers, for whatever reasons. And the CETA titles were oriented toward funding better, more effective services that might be determined best through competitive means. Even in DSS, the concern for cost has become a factor in recent years with budget constraints.

Competition

In this study the lack of meaningful competition in the services market was found to be a significant problem for the departments and reduced the possibility of meeting some of the other conditions. With only a small pool of agencies, officials were often forced to give contracts to the only available providers, even though they did not always conform to the government's priorities or, as under Title IV, they were expected to encounter administrative and service difficulties. Lack of competition in the services environment translated into lack of choice for DSS and BET. In addition, the donation requirement, the Title IV increasing match, the county role, and the narrow solicitation procedures all combined to reduce the departments' choices even further. These policies arose out of various federal and state goals that, in effect, worked at cross purposes with the goal of competition.

Rational Decision-Making Process

Outside suppliers were widely used in Title XX because of earlier political pressures to capture the available federal matching funds and private agencies' experience in a wide variety of specialized services. BET's reasons for using contracting out stemmed from both its lack of expertise and the policy goals for the state CETA programs—i.e., BET should merely coordinate programs and give contracts to community agencies that in time could be funded through local support. Thus, the departments did not use strictly *economically* rational reasons for choosing purchase; they chose contracting out for solid pragmatic and programmatic reasons.

Two different decision-making processes were obvious when the Michigan cases were compared. On the one hand, DSS used incremental, satisficing strategies to choose services and providers for Title XX. DSS usually awarded contract renewals routinely and chose contractors for their reputation and experience. Relationships between officials and contractors were generally cooperative, and close—except when contracts needed to be eliminated or cut. This approach lowered the administrative costs of contracting out (both to DSS and the agencies), but meant that DSS found it difficult to change service priorities, contractors, or funding levels. When it did make certain changes, both in services and in decentralization, they were gradual, incremental steps.

In contrast, at least for the Title II youth contracts, BET tried the classic rational, comprehensive approach to planning, solicitations, proposal evaluations, and award decisions. It made its choices on the basis of the proposals—to determine the design of the projects and the responsiveness to the RFP. It did not depend on feedback about current contracts to select agencies, but tried to select agencies with innovative approaches to serving its target populations. It set a three-year limit on awards, and, to encourage the continuation of successful programs, added an increasing match requirement. Its aims were frustrated, however, by certain realities—lack of competition in the service environment, intrusion of political influence, and the bureaucratic rule of expanding all appropriated funds. Consequently, the agencies generally did not perform their administrative and service tasks to BET's satisfaction. Moreover, both decision-making and start-up costs were high, such that BET did not expect to use the approach again.

Common to programs in both departments, however, were at least three major decision-making influences. First, the presence of political pressures have sometimes determined the awards and robbed the system of objectivity and fairness. In DSS, politicians, departments heads, and the Boards of Social Services have usually acted to *prevent* officials from reducing or ending a particular contract; while in BET, legislators and appointed officials have promoted certain public or private agencies for new awards. Either way, these political influences threatened the bureaucrats' professionalism, the service goals, and the fairness of the process.

Second, in both departments, the relative costs of competing proposals (if there was any direct competition) were seldom considered in granting awards. Service quality and expected effectiveness could be important, but only if there were similar agencies in direct competition — an infrequent occurrence in most DSS counties and under CETA's Title II. The departments did not try to optimize for the best quality, most effective services at the least cost level. They often had to choose the available agencies that could provide any kind of service for the clients. In these respects, DSS and BET contracting behavior did not conform to the conditional implications of contracting proponents.

Third, the decision-making process was marked by a fragmentation of contract authority in both cases. Although BET was more highly centralized in its organization, both departments gave different units pieces of responsibility for contracting out. Thus, policies were unclear, communication broke down, and tension arose among officials. In DSS, the county offices divided responsibility for various stages of the process among the program staff, the caseworkers, the contract coordinator (or services head), the Boards of Social Services, and the director. In addition, although the counties had been given some responsibility for their own contracts, the state program offices made policies affecting the contracts, and wrote their own contracts — even in counties where a contracts coordinator was hired. The contract management section was often at odds with both the counties and the program offices, since it was responsible for reviewing the contracts and budgets for compliance. In BET, the tensions between the policy and operations divisions arose because of the different goals and professional status of the program planners and the contract administrators. Not only did these factors increase the bureaucracy of the contracting system, but it also led to confusion for contractors concerning the actual roles of various participants.

The Watchdog Role

One of the weakest parts of the contracting process appears to be the reviews of expenditures, compliance, performance, and effectiveness for both DSS and BET programs. For the most part, the departments have not had adequate resources to monitor contractors and conduct periodic evaluations of their programs. Because of federal requirements, officials have independently monitored eligibility, but have depended upon contractors to supply information on other matters. Consumers of the services have had infrequent opportunities to express their needs, suggestions, and complaints.

In addition, DSS' and BET's watchdog roles have been rendered almost ineffective by other factors: 1) Michigan's attorney general ruled that contractors could not be held responsible for failure to meet performance goals; 2) information that the departments have obtained about compliance and performance often did not determine whether or not a renewal will be made, in view of service and political factors; and 3) frequently there were no other sources of supply that could meet the departments' and/or clients' needs. As a result, few mechanisms operated to ensure that contractors were producing the kinds of services and results desired by officials and needed by clients.

The Realities of Contracting Out

These findings about human services contracting in Michigan tend to agree with certain conclusions of the few other works about these services. Straussman and Farie found that in a large New York State county, few service providers competed for social services contracts.[1] They suggest that the organization of social services, the goal of service quality, and federal and state laws deterred competition and restricted the use of contracting out. The work of Kenneth R. Wedel and his associates emphasizes that the states' needs assessments, performance monitoring, and program effectiveness evaluations need major improvements to assist decision makers in making wise choices.[2] Both of these studies imply that the human services are very different from the hard services which have been more successfully purchased. Not only are the contracting systems for human services far more complex, but these services are also characterized by different goals, clients, and problems. A major issue raised by this study of Michigan human services was that the social and employment services were intended to be effective in changing the lives of clients—not only to give them some temporary service or assistance. Thus, the quality and effectiveness of services were generally more important than whether they cost less. In addition, the nonprofit agencies that were so critical in delivering these services operate under different pressures and incentives than do most profit-making firms, such as garbage collection companies. This difference must be recognized and explained to the extent that if contracting out is used, we can better understand the interorganizational and professional dynamics that drive a successful purchasing enterprise.

Beyond these immediate substantive conclusions, this study has broader theoretical implications because of what it suggests about contracting in general. The strength of the theoretical, comparative case study approach is that it illuminates not only the particular patterns of contracting, but it also can shed light on the applicability of the public choice perspective, the common features and problems of human service contracting, and some of the conditions under which contracting out may not meet certain efficiency goals. The major difficulty with the contracting prescription is that too often it is given as a panacea for the current ills of government with little explicit recognition of the requisite conditions and realities of implementation.

At least three general deficiencies have been evident in the public choice perspective on contracting out. First, contracting proponents have failed to recognize the critical role the service environment can play in contracting out, both in terms of the pool of potential providers and the input and feedback of service consumers. Not enough attention has been paid to the effect that government programs, regulations, and funds have had on creating contractors, encouraging government dependency, and giving critical advantages to certain providers. The fact that many of the human services are delivered to the powerless, inarticulate poor of society has meant that service needs and evaluations usually originate from suppliers and bureaucrats—not from the clients or their designated representatives.

Second, despite its major contributions to our understanding of public bureaucracy, the public choice school in its advocacy of contracting out has overlooked the motivational and organizational contexts of the contracting participants. Certain public choice scholars have shown that bureaucrats are motivated by self-interest that results in empire-building, budget maximization, and inefficiency. Although this view may be too simplistic, they have not applied this general understanding to the bureaucratic and political behaviors that determine the design, decisions, and, eventually, the outcomes of contracting systems. The obvious questions are: Why should bureaucratic and political behaviors change with contracting out? What incentives are there to achieve efficiency goals? We need to develop a more realistic understanding of the role and environment of contracting officials. As Phillip J. Cooper argues:

> . . . the major task of the contracting officials may be to balance political supports and demands in light of government needs and available resources rather than the frequently repeated goal of acquisition of the best goods and services at the lowest possible price.[3]

Third, until now the importance of the contracting organizational structure, process, and procedures has been virtually ignored in the public administration and economics literature. Too readily have some contracting advocates assumed that quasi-market mechanisms will automatically work wonders in providing services, without exploring how and why contracting out is actually utilized, what procedures are critical in producing the expected benefits, and under which constraints and inducements the various actors operate.

Contracting for human services is actually far more complex than might be expected from procontracting works. The process involves multiple participants whose actions are often uncoordinated and sometimes contradictory. In DSS, federal, state, and county units were responsible for specifying and interpreting Title XX (and sometimes state) regulations, particularly those dealing with purchase-of-service arrangements. In turn, these requirements had to be explained and applied to all the prospective providers, who, of course, had their own goals and procedures to follow. The need to provide technical assistance to contractors of both departments' programs was obvious during the contract proposal, writing, and implementation stages. This emphasis upon proper procedures clearly led to the phenomenon of 'goal displacement,' in which bureaucrats sought to achieve instrumental means (proper procedures and paperwork) almost to the exclusion of end goals—i.e., permanent employment and independence from government assistance for clients.

In other words, those who prescribe contracting out as a method of privatization have examined the subject in a rather narrow and simplistic way. From a theoretical point of view, contracting out does not mimic the market, and it creates additional bureaucratic problems. The realities of government mean that this alternative to traditional methods of supply is not an easy, clear-cut solution to governments' knotty problems.

These criticisms of the public choice perspective on contracting out are not meant to refute public choice theory itself, however. Rather, the universal application of the contracting prescription is being challenged. I have not contradicted those who claim that government is too big and that bureaucracy is often a clumsy vehicle for delivering services. I have not questioned some of the fundamental causal relationships that have been asserted by this perspective—that competition is the most effective way of cutting costs and improving services. Nor have I raised the legitimate question whether government *should* try to maximize efficiency in human services, or the related issue of whether slowing government growth through privatization is a desirable end in itself. These matters, however important, are beyond the scope of this work, but may prove to be fruitful areas of inquiry for others to address.

The question arises, then, if contracting out does not fulfill the efficiency goals claimed for it, what about other quasi-market mechanisms? Some public choice proponents could conclude that this study offers a solid reason why government bureaucracy and its complex process and regulations should be avoided altogether and vouchers, for example, that given directly to program recipients, would provide a better means for supplying human services and giving clients a choice. Such a conclusion would not necessarily be valid; one of the key problems with the human services is the need for *effective* services. How are clients, many of whom have few information resources and often lack adequate education, to understand the range of choices and their expected outcomes for themselves or their children?[4] In addition, as the BET case showed, private agencies may not be able to supply successful programs for those who pay by voucher. As Walter Williams asks: "What happens if schools 'sell' training that does not yield jobs, or businesses let people go after the wage subsidy period?"[5] Do we continue to pay for services that waste the taxpayers' money and clients' time? Government would have to establish a role even in these areas—for eligibility determinations, in informing clients of various options, for licensing or regulation of agencies, for reviews of effectiveness. Thus, in Williams' words, the " 'Law of markets' does not guarantee technical breakthroughs or yield an automatic solution to the immense organizational problems that bedevil complex social service delivery programs."[6]

The Three Alternative Perspectives

Now that the public choice perspective has been shown to be seriously deficient in describing, explaining, and predicting contracting behavior in these human services, what of the three alternative perspectives of market imperfections, cooptation, and organizational decision making? Which of these models is correct? The prevous chapters have shown that all three perspectives have something to contribute to our understanding of contracting out. By themselves, none of the perspectives offers a complete, accurate picture of the process and its problems. Each perspective draws our attention to different factors that explain certain aspects of the process, decisions, and outputs. These perspectives are not incompatible; they neatly mesh to provide a broader, more balanced view of purchasing human services.

The Economics of Market Imperfections

The perspective of market imperfections was particularly relevant and applicable to these cases of human service contracting. It rightly emphasized the problems and causes of inadequate competition in the environment and in procedures, as well as the significance of inadequate information in making awards and conducting reviews. Basic economic forces did shape many of the decisions and behaviors of contracting participants in both DSS and BET. Contracting out in these human services was marked by few competitors, a lack of competitive procedures in many cases, and dependence upon sellers' information and preferences. The research did not, however, discover signs of attempts at collusion, price setting, or market control, even though the human services system discourages direct competition.

The Politics of Cooptation

The cooptation perspective predicted some of the political influences that affect contracting decision making. Since they had intense material interests at stake, providers became more involved than clients and taxpayers in the planning and contracting process. Not only did their views shape decisions about service needs, but they also were successful in getting politicians and appointed officials to operate on their behalf when a contract was available or a renewal was threatened. Therefore, not all contractors were treated alike. Some, such as the public agencies in BET, were given special advantages over others, whether through their political ties, federal regulations, or bureaucratic, political, or professional relationships. Although the role of providers has not taken the extreme and highly organized forms found by cooptation scholars in some federal and state agencies, this perspective heightens our awareness of the possible problems that can arise out of contracting out.

The Process of Organizational Decision Making

This third alternative perspective probably was the most useful and insightful of the three alternative approaches—at least for these human services cases. It emphasized that contracting out takes place within an organization (or many organizations, actually) where officials have had limited resources with which to make choices about needs, awards, and reviews. In addition, since many actors and units participated in DSS and BET decisions, the process became very protracted and complex which, at times, produced conflicts and tensions. Broadening competition and choice through more extensive solicitations in BET and changing the donation requirement in one county DSS presented additional problems for the bureaucrats. The RFP process was costly, while increased competition created uncertainty and resentment among contractors.

In the face of these conditions, officials generally used shortcuts and satisficing strategies to make contracting policy, procedures, and award decisions. Granting renewals in DSS became commonplace. A key factor in decisions in both departments was a preference for professionalism, as evidenced in choosing contractors because of their professional reputations or for their ability to compile professional proposals that met the needs of BET. Usually, professional behavior by contractors meant that the quality of their work and services in DSS was judged to be good, despite the virtual absence of government review and other mechanisms to constrain their behavior. Thus, professionalism—not competition—was the key ingredient in producing services that were at least equal to or better than what DSS itself could provide. It is somewhat questionable as to how independently officials arrived at these judgments of quality. The fact that these reputable agencies were run by competent and specialized professionals with the correct education and affiliations could mean that officials concluded they must be producing good quality and effective services. However, it can be surmised that, sometimes, the common professional goals, methods, and biases served as a substitute for assessing the actual needs of clients and the actual outcomes of outside suppliers' services.

Throughout the contracting process, it was clear that various departmental, federal, and state policies were also instrumental in shaping contracting relationships and outcomes. Federal concern for client eligibility meant that DSS' and BET's scarce review resources were used primarily to check client abuses, not project effectiveness. Requirements for matching funds may have helped to prevent total dependence on one state contract and also may have been an indication of local or agency commitment to a program.

But it reduced competition and choice as well. In the DSS case, it meant that often officials could not match agencies with the critical needs of clients.

In addition, the more informal rules and characteristics of organizations generated some undesirable outcomes. The stated goals of the programs were often superceded by the operating goals of individuals, units, and the bureaucracy as a whole. Probably the most common bureaucratic norm was the need for departments to spend their entire appropriation each fiscal year, since strong disincentives existed to return unused funds. Consequently, the state DSS felt forced to write an eleventh-hour contract with an influential interest group association that represented family and child counseling agencies, since officials did not have the time to write separate contracts with several agencies before the deadline. In BET, officials were also compelled to write contracts with agencies that had submitted inadequate project proposals due to the need to spend their CETA allocation.

Because of organizational structures, differing goals, and professional norms, additional problems also surfaced. DSS tended to have conflicts about awards and oversight between state program staff and contract management personnel—between those concerned about proper procedure and those concerned about program design and content. These conflicts led to delays and consumption of already scarce staff and fiscal resources. BET's division between contract administrators and program staff led to inadequate communication about CETA requirements and to contractor confusion.

Finally, the interviews showed that not only were there problems in contracting out due to the public bureaucracy in its various levels and units, but that contractors also had their own bureaucracies—whether public or private. A few of the agencies, particularly the private ones, were fairly small, but many were as large as, or larger than, BET. Therefore, services were delivered through bureaucratic structures and rules anyway, and communication about proposals, awards, and reviews were filtered through *two* bureaucratic systems. Not only did this make the process more confusing for everyone, it also meant that lines of accountability were less clear and that the organizations' goals might conflict. Ultimately, these factors increased the costs of contracting out and caused participants to focus even more on the process, rather than the effectiveness, of purchasing services.

Conclusion

Where and when should contracting out be considered a viable alternative to in-house supply? To begin the process of identifying favorable conditions for contracting out more efficiently and effectively, the following tentative list offers some situations that have potential for implementing contracting out: where demonstration, experimental programs, services, or methods can be tried with no long-term commitment to continuing the programs; when there is a genuine, common need and desire to cut costs and maintain good quality services; where government does not have the requisite experience, equipment, or expertise to supply the service; when government needs certain services occasionally or seasonally; where economies of scale can be realized; where government officials can set priorities, service levels, and outcome goals, with the opportunity to reward and punish if these are not met by contractors; where there is adequate competition in the environment to ensure government choice; where fair competitive procedures can be adopted and enforced; where politically motivated awards can be minimized; where government agencies have the resources and desire to implement effective oversight methods. Obviously, all these conditions are not required to be present at the same time for contracting out to meet the public choice goals of contracting. In some cases, seemingly necessary conditions of contracting out can be absent if other compensating conditions are present.

In setting up these suitable conditions for contracting out, I have assumed the goals of the contracting advocates—least cost for the best quality services and a slowdown of government growth. Different observers of contracting out may not agree that these goals should be of primary importance throughout government. Other goals government may wish to maximize may also be met through contracting out, perhaps with different conditions. In part, the perceived success or failure of the system depends upon participants' goals and expectations of the service. In the human services examined here, the Michigan government primarily used the private sector for specialized services not normally available in the departments. It can be safely said for both cases that, compared to government delivery, the cost and quality of contracted services were probably not uniformly better or worse. However, if the support of private agencies for welfare issues can be bought with contracts and agreements, or if additional funds can be captured by this means, the purchasing approach may appear to be even more desirable. Although contracting out is usually recommended on efficiency grounds, it is clear that participants in and out of government were not primarily interested in cutting costs and improving service quality. They found other reasons for using this method. Due to different goals, they did not maximize traditional procurement principles. Rather, they were influenced by their professional and organizational systems to behave quite differently than that suggested by the public choice approach to contracting out.

This effort to identify the necessary conditions for successful contracting out has only begun with this limited study. Many other services, levels, and organizational environments should be examined to verify or change these conclusions and add to this attempt. This study has not been able to examine precisely the various cost and service outcomes of contracting in DSS and BET programs. Measuring costs and benefits of any program is difficult, but in contracting out, the task can be almost impossible for certain services. Just the same, such attempts could illuminate even more the relationships between the conditions and the outcomes, which have only been estimated in this work.

For the most part, throughout this study, I have viewed contracting out primarily through the eyes of the government. However, a growing literature, alluded to in the first chapter, focuses on the views of the contractors. This is an interesting and important area of study, for it can help to understand better how government contracting out affects these agencies. This sort of research will logically lead to grappling with another, fundamental question in public administration and political theory: What is the proper role of the state vis-à-vis private agencies and groups—particularly those that deliver public services? To use Bruce L.R. Smith and D.C. Hague's terms, this tension between private agency independence and government control continues to be a modern dilemma.[7]

CONCLUDING ANALYSIS OF CONDITIONS & PERSPECTIVES

Honest and thorough attempts at studying these various aspects of contracting out can go far to increase our knowledge of human behavior, organizations, and the interface between public and private sectors. Adding to our present information can assist scholars and practitioners in their understanding of the complexities of implementing government programs and management devices. By studying contracting we can learn how to alter conditions to achieve its positive benefits. However, changing some of the conditions found in this study of human services may be difficult, if not impossible, since certain problems (e.g., lack of adequate resources), at this time, seem almost insurmountable. In those cases, it may be wise to concede that neither public or private delivery of services can readily overcome the major problems. Yet, if contracting out is being considered and employed more frequently during times of fiscal strain, it would also be wise to understand, anticipate, and compensate for the problems that are likely to arise.

Appendix A

Methods of Study

For this study, both the unstructured, personal interview approach and the interview schedule offered distinctive advantages over the questionnaire as a research tool; therefore, they were used to obtain much of the information about the contracting process and opinions from approximately sixty individuals. A seasoned political researcher, Lewis Anthony Dexter, argues that the interview method is especially appropriate when trying to obtain complete information from elite or specialized individuals—particularly where the researcher is uncertain of all the dimensions of the subject.[1] This approach dovetailed with my more exploratory endeavor. In addition, according to others, the interview format allows the interviewer the opportunity to control the administration setting, to interpret complex questions correctly for the interviewee, to prod for further clarification or examples, to evaluate the validity of the information, and to ensure that the interviewee considers the questions seriously.[2] The result is more relevant, accurate, and wholistic information than that obtained through a questionnaire. Since my research goals and available sources largely necessitated qualitative, rather than quantitative, methods of study, I employed the interview schedule as a mainstay of my research.

Because the results of interviews in most cases are only as good as the interviewer and the interview schedule, particular attention was paid to developing a standardized schedule and standardized interview style to reduce interviewer variations. I conducted all interviews myself with a pretested interview schedule that used the terminology familiar to all respondents. Because of prepared multiple alternatives and the complexity of some questions, the interviewees were asked to follow the questions on their copy of the schedule while I recorded their answers on a separate copy. If the use of a prepared schedule did not eliminate all possible biases due to expectations of the interviewees' opinions, the schedule, at least, reduced possibilities for differential errors in asking, probing, and recording responses.

In setting up the interview appointment and beginning the interview, I always stressed that I was working on an independent research project about contracting out for services in public administration. The need for this approach was frequently made obvious by queries about my use of information that was not complimentary about interviewees' units, other bureaucrats, or politicians. I explained to both state officials and contractors that I had received approval for the research project from department authorities, but that their answers were confidential. Interviewees were promised that neither their identities, positions, or organizations would be reported to other officials or in any published accounts. With only a few exceptions, I considered I was successful in achieving good, trusting relationships with interviewees. (And those with whom I did not develop a good rapport were generally cooperative in answering the questions.) To prevent biasing the results, I did not communicate anything about the theoretical perspectives, their expectations, or my working hypotheses on contracting out, even though I was often asked my personal opinion about the subject.

The content of the interview schedule was important in establishing credibility and rapport with interviewees. The format and questions were based on the initial interviews and pretests with public officials, as well as my own background knowledge. As a result, the respondents had little difficulty understanding and answering the questions.

The interview schedule was designed to examine the procedures of contracting out and the viewpoints of those most involved in the process—state and county officials and contractors. This information was crucial in evaluating the theoretical perspectives and accomplishing the research goal of including the significant advantages and disadvantages associated with human services contracting. The schedule itself had three parts, in the following order: 1) personal background questions (e.g., education, previous positions); 2) questions about the process of contracting (from solicitation procedures to award protests); and 3) opinion and attitude questions (e.g., problems in their work, contracting out in general). (See Appendix B.) A variety of question formats was used, including open-ended questions, fixed alternatives with probes, and graphic rating scales. Lewis Anthony Dexter, among others, has stated that biases in wording and subject acquiescence are less of a problem in interviewing elites than in most public opinion surveying; nonetheless, attention was paid to developing questions and fixed alternatives that minimized these problems.[3] Many of the questions were open-ended or included probes that

146   CONTRACTING OUT FOR HUMAN SERVICES

allowed the interviewee to explain or restate an answer. While it was important to establish my credibility and interest in the subject, it was just as necessary to make clear to the respondents that I was open to being 'taught' about how contracting out really was, in their own words.

Three different interview schedules were used with three different groups in both the Department of Labor and the Department of Social Services. The main schedule, which included all three sections of questions, was administered to the major state and county officials in the departments, in interviews from ninety minutes to three and a half hours. Because of time constraints, four forty-five to sixty minute interviews were also conducted, using a shortened form consisting of the sections on personal backgrounds and opinions. Such questions illuminated differences and similarities among the various types of contracting officials.

A third interview schedule was developed for service providers. Where possible, the same questions were incorporated or slightly reworded to provide points of comparison between the public officials and the contractors. Several procedural questions were used to check the answers of the public officials to determine if contractors actually observed some regulations put into practice in the form the bureaucrats said they were. Some additional questions were designed specifically for the contractors. These interviews were mainly conducted at the agencies and took between one and two hours to conduct.

The selection of interviewees was the next preinterview step in the research. In both DSS and BET, most of the major programmatic and contracting officials were selected for interviews (four each from DSS and DOL), plus about twenty percent of the contract specialists (two from each department). In DSS, the selection process was complicated by the significant role of the counties in contracting out. To include county perspectives, seven contract supervisors in counties where private contractors were used to deliver client services were interviewed. Of the eighty-three Michigan counties, only some contract for services, and only seven employed a full-time contracts coordinator. As a result, mainly the larger, contracting counties were included in the sample. Nonetheless, the state officials who made state contracts and who had statewide jurisdictions gave me additional information about the other, smaller counties.

Private service contractors were also selected for interviews from department lists of current and past contractors. The resulting contractor sample with ten providers associated with each department may not have been representative of the population, since they were not strictly randomly selected. However, some variety in the types of services, the target groups, and the location of the agencies was achieved.

In contacting public officials and contractors for interviews, I met with moderate success. I had the approval of the evaluation division head in DSS and BET's deputy directors helped to open doors, but I was unable to talk with all the people I had wanted to due to department-imposed limits on the sample size. This kept down the size of the sample, but by careful selection of interviewees both in the early stages and the interview schedule phase, I was able to obtain an informative mix of respondents.

One of the problems with this research plan is the lack of random sampling. The choice of respondents was determined by their available time, departmental approval, and my own criteria for services and service providers. What may allow me to claim some representativeness in analyzing the programs is that such large percentages of the populations were usually interviewed—usually around fifty percent. The lack of a large or random county sample in DSS was dictated by the fact that only some counties contract out with private sources for many services. As a result, those county contract supervisors interviewed were actually a sample of a limited population of contracting counties. I limited my interviews to counties with at least two client service contracts under the donated funds approach. I included three of the four largest, most highly urbanized counties in the state in the sample because they had large numbers of contracts. However, two smaller counties with only two and three contracts also were included.

An additional difficulty was encountered in choosing appropriate research and statistical methods as well as the size of the sample. The unit of analysis under examination was not entirely clear. It is the individual respondent, the contract, the program, the service, or the department? Relatively little quantitative research has been done in similar areas, perhaps in part because of this issue. A related problem in this type of research is that all individuals cannot be analyzed equally about more objective purchasing procedures, because of different levels of knowledge about the contracting process. In both respects, then, employing quantitative methods to add up, compare, and anlyze responses would not produce a thorough, in depth analysis of contracting out. Although my intent before I conducted the preliminary open-ended interviews had been to try to quantify responses, I soon discovered, as Donald Warwick did in his organizational research, that more qualitative methods were most appropriate and provided a richness not found in quantitative data analysis.[4]

Notes

1. *Elite and Specialized Interviewing* (Evanston, IL: Northwestern University Press, 1970).

2. Raymond L. Gorden, *Interviewing: Strategy, Techniques, and Tactics* (Homewood, IL: Dorsey Press, 1969), 52-54.
3. Dexter, *Elite and Specialized Interviewing,* pp. 5-24.
4. Donald P. Warwick, *A Theory of Public Bureaucracy: Politics, Personality, and Organization in the State Department* (Cambridge, MA: Harvard University Press, 1975).

Appendix B

Service Contract Interview Schedule

In this interview, I am interested in learning more about service contracting in the state of Michigan in general, and in your area of contracting in particular. Not only do I want to know more factual information about the process, but I would also like to hear your point of view and opinions about your work. Therefore, many questions will not have a strictly right or wrong answer, since people see things differently. I assure you that the responses you give will be kept confidential. Your answers to all questions will be used for research purposes only and will not be identified with your name or position. In the interest of time, please try to keep your answers short and to the point.

A. Background Questions

    1. To be completed by interviewer:
        For bureaucrats—department of employment:
        ____1. Labor
        ____2. Social Services—state
        ____3. Social Services—county
        Contractual program affiliated with:

    2. Job of Respondent:
        ____1. contract specialist
        ____2. contract supervisor
        ____3. program specialist
        ____4. program supervisor
        ____5. section chief
        ____6. program evaluator

       ____7. contractor
       ____8. other (specify)
- a. Number of years in this unit?
- b. Age of respondent:
    - ____1. 21-30
    - ____2. 31-40
    - ____3. 41-50
    - ____4. 51-60
    - ____5. 61-70
- c. Highest level of education completed:
    - ____1. high school
    - ____2. some college
    - ____3. 4-year college degree
    - ____4. Master's degree
    - ____5. some graduate school
    - ____6. Ph.D.
    - ____7. some other graduate degree (specify)

Major area of study in college or graduate school:
- ____1. public administration
- ____2. social work
- ____3. law
- ____4. business
- ____5. social sciences
- ____6. humanities
- ____7. other (specify)

3. a. From which of the following private sources do you (or your unit) purchase services by contract: (may check more than one)
    - ____1. private, nonprofit agencies
    - ____2. private, proprietary (profit-making) agencies or companies
    - ____3. public agencies
   b. What are the names of some of your largest contractors, and the amounts of their current contracts?

B. Descriptive Process Questions

4. Which of the following agencies or departments must approve *all* contracts from your unit?
    - ____1. Department of Management and Budget
    - ____2. Office of the attorney general
    - ____3. Civil Service Department
    - ____4. Civil Rights Department

APPENDIX B   151

    ____5. House & Senate Fiscal Agencies or Appropriations Committees
    ____6. none of the above
    ____7. some other agency/department (specify)

5. Which of the following agencies or departments must approve *some* of the contracts from your unit?
   ____1. Department of Management and Budget
   ____2. Office of the attorney general
   ____3. Civil Service Department
   ____4. Civil Rights Department
   ____5. House and Senate Fiscal Agencies or Appropriations Committees
   ____6. none of the above
   ____7. some other agency/department (specify)

6. In your program areas, how is it usually decided that a project or program will be provided through the private sector rather than by public employees? (may choose more than one)
   ____1. by state statute
   ____2. by state Constitution
   ____3. by federal laws or regulations
   ____4. by department policy
   ____5. by program heads
   ____6. by some other means (specify)
   ____7. don't know

7. Approximately how many contracts have you *personally* worked on in the last fiscal year (1980)?

8. Approximately how many contracts were drawn up or processed in the last calendar year in the program area of _____?

9. How are potential contractors informed of a particular project or program that your department will purchase from a private source? (may check more than one)
   ____1. newspapers
   ____2. trade or professional newsletter or magazines
   ____3. posted notices in state offices
   ____4. letter
   ____5. other means (specify)

10. If only some contractors are notified:
    a. How is it decided which contractors will be notified?
    b. How many contractors are usually notified in your area?

11. Are specific solicitation instruments required to purchase contracted services in your area of work?
    ____1. yes
    ____2. no
    ____3. sometimes
    a. *If yes*, which of the following is (are) necessary? (may check more than one)
       ____1. Request for Proposal (RFP)
       ____2. Request for Quote (RFQ)
       ____3. letter of intent
       ____4. other solicitation instrument (specify)
    b. *if sometimes*, under what circumstances are they required?
       If a solicitation instrument is *sometimes* necessary, which of the following is used?
       ____1. Request for Proposal (RFP)
       ____2. Request for Quote (RFQ)
       ____3. letter of intent
       ____4. other solicitation instrument (specify)
12. When soliciting bids or programs from private sources, does your office explicitly state that certain requirements must be met by the contractor?
    ____1. yes
    ____2. no
    ____3. sometimes
    a. *if yes*, what kinds of requirements are explicitly stated?
       ____1. cost
       ____2. equal opportunity employment
       ____3. affirmative action program
       ____4. length of the contract (time period)
       ____5. specifications about quality of service provided
       ____6. specifications about number of clients/recipients to be served
       ____7. other performance specifications
       ____8. other kinds of requirements (specify)
    b. *if sometimes*, under what circumstances are requirements stated?
       If requirements are sometimes stated, what kinds are they? (see list above in 12.a. No. 1-8)
13. When bids or proposals are invited, are the criteria by which

proposals will be evaluated included in the package or notice?
- ____1. yes
- ____2. no
- ____3. sometimes

If sometimes, under what circumstances are they included?

14. When a bid or proposal for a program is solicited, are contractor review methods and criteria included in the notice?
    - ____1. yes
    - ____2. no
    - ____3. sometimes

    If sometimes, under what circumstances are they included?

15. Is a budget included with the contractor's proposal?
    - ____1. always
    - ____2. usually
    - ____3. sometimes
    - ____4. never

    If usually or sometimes, under what circumstances would a budget be submitted?

16. Must the contractor's proposal, including work plan and bid prices or proposal amounts, meet *all requirements* contained in the original solicitation notice in order to be considered for a contract?
    - ____1. yes
    - ____2. no
    - ____3. sometimes

    If no or sometimes, which requirements are usually more flexible, and why?

17. Who evaluates contractor proposals in your program area? (may check more than one)
    - ____1. department contract administrator (central office)
    - ____2. contract officer in program division, section, or unit (circle one)
    - ____3. a panel of evaluators in program division, section, or unit
    - ____4. some other group or individual (specify)

    If a panel is used, what are their usual positions in the department?

18. Do these individuals know which contractors have submitted which proposals?
    ____1. always
    ____2. sometimes
    ____3. never

19. In your area of service contracting, how frequently does your unit receive *unsolicited* proposals for programs or projects?
    ____1. often
    ____2. sometimes
    ____3. never
    ____4. don't know

20. As a result of an unsolicited proposal, how frequently does the proposing source receive a contract for the service they wish to perform?
    ____1. always
    ____2. often
    ____3. sometimes
    ____4. never
    ____5. don't know

21. In your program area, how frequently are contracts negotiated between contracting officials and contractors, instead of through the competitive bidding process?
    ____1. always
    ____2. usually
    ____3. sometimes
    ____4. never
    Why are they negotiated? Which parts of the contract are most negotiable?

22. Is competitive bidding always, sometimes or never required in your program area?
    ____1. always
    ____2. sometimes
    ____3. never
    a. *If sometimes*, when is competitive bidding required?
    b. *If competitive bidding* is used, is there a specified policy that requires award of a contract to the lowest bidder, provided minimum specifications are met?
       ____1. yes
       ____2. no

23. In the contracted projects or programs you are acquainted with

in your division, how many different contractors' bids or proposals are usually considered before an award is made?

24. In your program area, is a written proposal or an oral presentation required before the decision is made on who will receive a contract? (may check more than one)
　　　____1. written proposal
　　　____2. oral presentation
　　　____3. neither is required, but one of the two is sometimes done
　　　____4. neither is required, so neither is done

25. On what basis is it decided that a certain firm or agency will receive a contract in your program area? (rank order the following reasons)
　　　____1. lowest cost
　　　____2. previous satisfactory work in state projects or services
　　　____3. adequate staff and equipment to do the job
　　　____4. previous experience in this general type of service
　　　____5. plan to fulfill all criteria provided in solicitation package
　　　____6. well-reasoned arguments why program elements will accomplish the desired goals, as given in the proposal
　　　____7. some other reason (specify)

26. When considering various bids or proposals for a contract, how important is it that the contractor be of a racial minority group?
　　　____1. very important
　　　____2. somewhat important
　　　____3. sometimes can be important
　　　____4. not very important
　　　____5. not at all important
    Does your unit keep track of how many minority contractors are awarded contracts?
　　　____1. yes
　　　____2. no

27. Are sole source contracts used in your program area?
　　　____1. yes
　　　____2. no
　　　____3. sometimes
   a. *If yes*, why is it used? Are there any restrictions on its use?
   b. *If sometimes*, under what circumstances is it used?

28. In the contracts you work with, which of the following items are always, sometimes, or never included in the contracts?

	always	sometimes	never
____1. limitations on employee wage/salary increases	1	2	3
____2. limitations on contractor administrative costs	1	2	3
____3. minimum wages for employees	1	2	3
____4. limitations on employees' overtime and compensatory time	1	2	3
____5. maximum wage/salary rates for major positions	1	2	3

29. In the cases of for-profit firms, are there standard fee scales or limitations on profit margins?
    ____1. yes
    ____2. no
    ____3. sometimes
    If there are, what are they?

30. In your area, do the contracts usually state that payments to contractors will be in specified lump-sum amounts, according to per-unit rates, or to reimburse approved costs?
    ____1. lump-sum amounts
    ____2. per-unit rates
    ____3. reimburse approved costs
    ____4. reimburse approved costs plus a specified fee
    ____5. some other form (specify)

31. Do any of the contractors awarded contracts in your area in turn subcontract for some or all of the services?
    ____1. yes
    ____2. no
    a. *If yes,* what types of agencies or firms subcontract? (may choose more than one, but rank in terms of frequency)
        ____1. private, non-profit agencies
        ____2. private, proprietary (for-profit) firms
        ____3. public agencies
    b. What types of firms receive subcontracts?

          ____1. private, non-profit agencies
          ____2. private, proprietary firms
          ____3. public agencies
     c. What role does your unit have in subcontracting? (may check more than one)
          ____1. provides guidelines for contractors to follow
          ____2. sets strict rules governing subcontracting
          ____3. helps to select subcontractors
          ____4. examines contracts
          ____5. reviews budgets for subcontractors
          ____6. checks to ensure that subcontractors are in compliance with EOE standards
          ____7. no role at all
          ____8. some other role (specify)
32. During the time you have worked in this unit, have any contracts been revoked or terminated before the specified end of the contract?
          ____1. yes
          ____2. no
     a. *If yes,* why were they revoked or terminated?
     b. How many contracts have been revoked or terminated while you have worked here?
     c. Approximately what percentage of the total number of contracts awarded in this area is that?
33. Have any firms or agencies been suspended or debarred from

          ____1. yes
          ____2. no
     a. *If yes,* how many?
     b. *If yes,* why?)
34. Is there a formal process for hearing contractor complaints in your contract area?
          ____1. yes
          ____2. no
     a. *If yes,* where can a contractor go if he/she has a complaint about the award of a contract?
     b. If a contractor has a complaint about regulations or payments for services, to whom can he/she go?
     c. What authority does the official have to change decisions about contracts, regulations, or payments?
     d. Approximately how many complaints have been regis-

tered concerning contracts in your area during the time you have worked here?

35. What kinds of review procedures are used in your program area for contracted services? (may check more than one)
    ____1. preaudit
    ____2. continuous monitoring of expenditures
    ____3. progress reports on performance or work accomplished
    ____4. on-site field monitoring of programs or projects
    ____5. in depth evaluations
    ____6. postaudit of expenditures
    ____7. postaudit/review of performance
    ____8. some other review procedure (specify)
  a. Which of these review methods are required of all contracts?
  b. Are any of these used for subcontracted services?
  c. If an in depth evaluation is done, who does it?
    ____1. the department evaluation unit
    ____2. an independent evaluator
    ____3. another state agency or department
    ____4. some other evaluation source (specify)
  d. Why would an in depth evaluation be done?
  e. If a postaudit is done, who does it?
    ____1. another state agency or department
    ____2. a departmental unit
    ____3. an independent accounting firm
    ____4. some other audit source (specify)

36. What do you believe is the *major* problem in monitoring and evaluating contractor performance?

37. In your department, are there any advisory boards, commissions, or councils that have a role in the contracted services you work with?
    ____1. yes
    ____2. no
  a. What are their names?
  b. Who are on these bodies?
  c. How are they appointed?
  d. Why was this advisory body formed?
  e. What is their role in the contracted programs and projects?

38. What are the major groups or associations that are active in your area of contracting? (specify with names)
    a. Who do they represent?
    b. How many members is that?
39. Are there any client, recipient, or consumer groups that contact you or others in your section about contracted programs or projects?
    ____1. yes
    ____2. no
    a. Please specify with names of organizations.
    b. Who do they represent?
    c. What is the size of their membership?
40. How are your contracts funded? (may check more than one)
    ____1. through federal grants
    ____2. through donated funds from private sources
    ____3. through donated funds from public sources
    ____4. through the general division's appropriation from the state legislature
    ____5. through a specific appropriation from the legislature for the contracted services alone
    ____6. some other source (specify)
    a. *If through federal grants*, specify program and title.
    b. *If through private donated funds*, specify the donors.
    c. *If through public donated funds*, specify the donors.
41. Approximately how much money will be spent this FY for contracted services in your section of _____?

C. Opinion Questions
    42. In general, how much say or influence do you think the people or agencies listed below have over *whether* a contract is made for a service with a private agency?

	None	Little	Moder. Amount	Great Deal	Very Great
____ 1. Civil Service-contracts divis.	1	2	3	4	5
____ 2. Office of the Attorney General	1	2	3	4	5
____ 3. The Civil Rights Department	1	2	3	4	5

160 CONTRACTING OUT FOR HUMAN SERVICES

_____ 4. Dept. of Management & Budget   1   2   3   4   5
_____ 5. Your department director   1   2   3   4   5
_____ 6. Department deputy director(s)   1   2   3   4   5
_____ 7. Bureau chief   1   2   3   4   5
_____ 8. Division chief   1   2   3   4   5
_____ 9. Section chief   1   2   3   4   5
_____10. Program specialists   1   2   3   4   5
_____11. Contract specialists   1   2   3   4   5
_____12. Private organizations   1   2   3   4   5
_____13. State legislature   1   2   3   4   5
_____14. Yourself   1   2   3   4   5

43. In general, how much say or influence do you think the people or agencies listed below have over *who* receives a contract in your own area?

_____ 1. Your department director   1   2   3   4   5
_____ 2. Department deputy director(s)   1   2   3   4   5
_____ 3. Bureau chief   1   2   3   4   5
_____ 4. Division chief   1   2   3   4   5
_____ 5. Section chief   1   2   3   4   5
_____ 6. Program specialists   1   2   3   4   5
_____ 7. Contract specialists   1   2   3   4   5
_____ 8. Private organizations   1   2   3   4   5
_____ 9. State legislators   1   2   3   4   5
_____10. Panel of proposal evaluators   1   2   3   4   5
_____11. Yourself   1   2   3   4   5

44. In your area of work, what have been the major problems with contracting with private agencies or firms for services?

APPENDIX B   161

45. In the contracts and services you work with, do you think contracting with private agencies or firms costs less than, about the same as, or more than, government delivery of those services would?
    ____1. less than government delivery
    ____2. about the same as government delivery
    ____3. more than government delivery
    ____4. don't have any idea

46. *In general,* for a wide variety of state services, do you think contracting with private agencies or firms costs less than, about the same as, or more than government delivery of those services?
    ____1. less than government delivery
    ____2. about the same as government delivery
    ____3. more than government delivery
    ____4. don't have any idea

47. For the contracts and services you work with, do you think contracting with private agencies or firms results in poorer service, about the same quality of service, or better service for recipients than government service delivery would?
    ____1. poorer service
    ____2. about the same quality
    ____3. better service
    ____4. don't have any idea

48. *In general,* for a wide variety of state services, do you think contracting with private agencies or firms results in poorer service, about the same quality of service, or better service for recipients than government service delivery would?
    ____1. poorer service
    ____2. about the same quality of service
    ____3. better service
    ____4. don't have any idea

49. Rank the following in order of importance (from 1 to 6, with 1 being the most important) as to why the private sector is used to supply public services in your program area instead of state (or county) public employees.
    ____1. lower cost
    ____2. better services
    ____3. greater flexibility in hiring and firing
    ____4. better oversight over cost and performance

___5. mandated by federal or state laws or regulations
___6. a way of strengthening private agencies or firms
___7. some other reason(s)

50. Use the following terms to describe your own relationships with contractors in your work:

	Always	Often	Sometimes	Never
___1. close and personal	1	2	3	4
___2. warm and friendly	1	2	3	4
___3. strictly businesslike	1	2	3	4
___4. cool and distant	1	2	3	4
___5. hostile and antagonistic	1	2	3	4

51. Do you believe that using private contractors to produce and deliver public services is somehow more democratic or less democratic than using public employees?
    ___1. more democratic
    ___2. less democratic
    ___3. doesn't have anything to do with democratic ideals
    Why?

52. In your area, do you believe that the monitoring and evaluation of contractors is:
    ___1. too strict, with too much unnecessary and burdensome paperwork involved
    ___2. not adequate to oversee expenditures
    ___3. not adequate to evaluate performance
    ___4. not strict enough to oversee expenditures *or* to evaluate performance adequately
    ___5. just about right
    ___6. some other response

53. In your experience in contracting, how do you evaluate the role of most politicians (e.g., state legislators, county commissioners, city councilmen) in the contracting process?
    ___1. generally quite helpful
    ___2. not involved enough in contracting
    ___3. too interfering in decision making
    ___4. hardly involved in contracting at all, but that's the way I prefer it

_____5. only involved in contracts that their constituents want, but otherwise hardly involved at all
_____6. some other response(s)

54. How frequently do you see yourself acting as an advocate for service providers in your work? (e.g., as with other state officials)
    _____1. always
    _____2. often
    _____3. sometimes
    _____4. never

55. In your area of contracting, if two units disagree over procedures, awards, etc., how are these conflicts resolved?

    In what matters are disagreements more likely between units or between various individuals involved in contracting?

56. What are the major problems you see in the relationship between the state department and the county?

57. What are the major problems or tensions *in your own job*, at least as it relates to contracting for services?

Notes

Chapter One

1. See John L. Palmer and Isabel V. Sawhill, eds., *The Reagan Experiment* (Washington, DC: Urban Institute, 1982), especially chapter 7.

2. James T. Bennett and Manuel H. Johnson, *Better Government at Half the Price* (Ottawa, IL: Carolina House, 1981).

3. E. S. Savas, *Privatizing the Public Sector* (Chatham, NJ: Chatham House, 1982).

4. Robert W. Poole, Jr., *Cutting Back City Hall* (New York: Universe Books, 1980).

5. Several different types of contracts and different ways of granting them have been used in many kinds of service areas. I will not, however, include consideration of financial agreements that are sometimes confused with contracts, such as grants-in-aid to lower levels of government, vouchers, research grants, or subsidies.

6. Donald Fisk, Herbert Kiesling, and Thomas Muller, *Private Provision of Public Services: An Overview* (Washington, DC: The Urban Institute, 1978).

7. See especially Gary J. Miller, *Politics of Municipal Incorporation* (Cambridge, MA: MIT Press, 1981); Sidney Sonenblum, John J. Kirlin, and John C. Ries, *How Cities Provide Services: An Evaluation of Alternative Delivery Structures* (Cambridge, MA: Ballinger Publications, 1977); Robert O. Warren, *Government in Metropolitan Regions: A Reappraisal of Fractionated Political Organization* (Davis, CA: Institute of Governmental Affairs, 1966).

8. See, for example, Clarence Danhof, *Government Contracting and*

Technological Change (Washington, DC: The Brookings Institution, 1968).

9. Bruce L. R. Smith, *The New Political Economy* (New York: St. Martin's Press, 1975), 1.

10. See especially Patricia S. Florestano and Stephen B. Gordon, "Public vs. Private: Small Government Contracting with the Private Sector," *Public Administration Review* 40 (Jan./Feb. 1980): 29-34; Jeffrey D. Straussman, "More Bang for Fewer Bucks? Or How Local Governments Can Rediscover the Potentials (and Pitfalls) of the Market," *Public Administration Review* 41 (Special Issue, 1981): 150-7; Poole, *Cutting Back.*

11. In the area of social services, see, for example, Neil Gilbert, "The Transformation of Social Services," *Social Service Review* 51 (December 1977): 624-41.

12. Probably the most relevant and representative works include James T. Bennett and Manuel H. Johnson, *Better Government*; Thomas E. Borcherding, ed., *Budgets and Bureaucrats: The Sources of Government Growth* (Durham, NC: Duke University Press, 1977); Vincent Ostrom and Elinor Ostrom, "Public Goods and Public Choices," in E. S. Savas, ed., *Alternatives for Delivering Public Services Toward Improved Performance* (Boulder, CO: Westview Press 1977), 7-49; Ostrom and Ostrom, "Public Choice: A Different Approach to the Study of Public Administration," *Public Administration Review* 31 (March/April 1971): 302-16; William A. Niskanen, Jr., *Bureaucracy and Representative Government* (Chicago: Aldine-Atherton, 1971); E. S. Savas, "Municipal Monopolies versus Competition in Delivering Urban Services," in Willis D. Hawley and David Rogers, eds., *Improving the Quality of Urban Management* (Beverly Hills, CA: Sage, 1974), 473-500; E. S. Savas, *Privatizing the Public Sector: How to Shrink Government* (Chatham, N.J.: Chatham House, 1982); Sonenblum et al., *How Cities Provide Services*; Gordon Tullock, *The Politics of Bureaucracy* (Washington, DC: Public Affairs Press, 1965).

13. Indeed some of these scholars might appropriately be classified as part of the more normative, rather than positive, school of public choice, and as such, tend to use a more ideological tone. See Dennis C. Mueller, *Public Choice* (Cambridge, UK: Cambridge University Press, 1979), especially Chapter 8. Because of their appointments in the Reagan administration, public choice scholars Roger Ahlbrandt, Jr., William A. Niskanen, Jr., and E. S. Savas have particularly been in positions to encourage the use of alternative service delivery mechanisms.

14. Niskanen, *Bureaucracy*; Bennett and Johnson, *Better Government*; Borcherding, *Budgets and Bureaucrats.*

15. Straussman, "More Bang." Also see the classic work on vouchers,

Milton Friedman, *Capitalism and Freedom* (Chicago: University of Chicago Press, 1972).

16. Savas, "Municipal Monopolies."

17. Lyle C. Fitch, "Increasing the Role of the Private Sector in Providing Public Services," in Willis D. Hawley and David Rogers, eds., *Improving the Quality of Urban Management* (Beverly Hills, CA: Sage, 1974), 264-306; Bennett and Johnson, *Better Government*; Niskanen, *Bureaucracy*; Savas, "Municipal Monopolies"; Robert M. Spann, "Public versus Private Provision of Governmental Services," in Borcherding, ed., *Budgets and Bureaucrats*; Dennis R. Young, "Institutional Change and the Delivery of Urban Public Services," *Policy Sciences* 2 (December 1971): 425-38.

18. Hirschman, *Exit, Voice, and Loyalty* (Cambridge, MA: Harvard University Press, 1970).

19. In particular, the Borcherding volume addresses this issue.

20. "Why Does Government Grow?" in Borcherding, *Budgets and Bureaucrats*.

21. Fisk, et al, *Private Provision*; Florestano and Gordon, "Public vs. Private."

22. Roger S. Ahlbrandt, Jr., "Efficiency in the Provision of Fire Services," *Public Choice* 18 (Fall 1973): 1-15.

23. David G. Davies, "The Efficiency of Public versus Private Firms: The Case of Australia's Two Airlines," *Journal of Law and Economics* 14 (April, 1971): 149-65.

24. Louis De Alessi, "An Economic Analysis of Government Ownership and Regulation: Theory and the Evidence from the Electric Power Industry," *Public Choice* 19 (Fall, 1974): 1-42.

25. Savas, "Solid Waste Collection in Metropolitan Areas," in Elinor Ostrom, ed., *The Delivery of Urban Services* (Beverly Hills, CA: Sage, 1976), 201-29, as well as other works by this author; Bennett and Johnson, "Public Versus Private Provision of Collective Goods and Services: Garbage Collection Revisited," *Public Choice* 34 (1979): 55-64; Peter Kemper and John M. Quigley, *The Economics of Refuse Collection* (Cambridge, MA: Ballinger, 1976).

26. Robert T. Deacon, "The Expenditure Effects of Alternative Public Supply Institutions," *Public Choice* 34 (1979): 381-397.

27. David Lowery, "The Political Incentives of Government Contracting," *Social Science Quarterly* 63 (September 1982): 517-529.

28. These include Davies, "The Efficiency of Public"; De Alessi, "An Economic Analysis"; Bennett and Johnson "Public Versus Private."

29. Deacon, "The Expenditure Effects;" Sonenblum, Kirlin, and Ries,

How Cities Provide Services; Warren, *Government in Metropolitan Regions*.

30. For a review of the basic organizational forms used in garbage collection, and a major study of cost comparisons among them, see E. S. Savas, Barbara J. Stevens, and Eileen B. Berenyi, "Solid Waste Collection: Organization and Efficiency of Service Delivery," Judith V. May and Aaron B. Wildavsky, eds., *The Policy Cycle* (Beverly Hills, CA: Sage, 1978), 145-165.

31. "Intracity Competition Between Public and Private Service Delivery," *Public Administration Review* 41 (Jan./Feb. 1981): 46-52.

32. "Tax Reduction Without Sacrifice: Private-Sector Production of Public Services," *Public Finance Quarterly* 8 (Oct. 1980): 363-96.

33. Douglas W. Ayres, "Municipal Interfaces in the Third Sector: A Negative View," *Public Administration Review* 35 (Sept./Oct. 1975): 459-63; John Hanrahan, *Government for $ale: Contracting Out—The New Patronage* (Washington, DC: American Federation of State, County, and Municipal Employees, 1977).

34. See Bennett and Johnson, "Public Versus Private."

35. Savas, *The Organization and Efficiency of Solid Waste Collection* (Lexington, MA: Lexington Books, 1977); Bennett and Johnson, "Public Versus Private."

36. Lowery, "The Political Incentives."

37. Bennett and Johnson, *Better Government*; Poole, *Cutting Back*; Savas, *Privatizing the Public Sector*.

38. Barbara J. Nelson, "Purchase of Services," in George Washnis, ed., *Productivity Improvement Handbook for State and Local Governments* (Washington, DC: National Academy of Public Administration, 1980), 427-47; Jeffrey D. Straussman and John Farie, "Contracting for Social Services at the Local Level," *Urban Interest p*(Spring, 1981): 43-50.

39. Straussman and Farie, "Contracting for Social Services," examined social service contracting in one New York county. Other, more policy-oriented overviews of social services include: Kenneth R. Wedel, Arthur J. Katz, and Ann Weick, eds., *Social Services by Government Contract: A Policy Analysis* (New York: Praeger, 1979); and Dennis R. Young and Richard R. Nelson, eds., *Public Policy for Day Care of Young Children* (Lexington, MA: Lexington Books, 1973).

40. Donald F. Kettl, "The Fourth Face of Federalism," *Public Administration Review* 41 (May/June 1981): 366-371.

41. Several scholars have begun to explore this important subject from various approaches, including Estelle James, "How Nonprofits Grow: A Model," *Journal of Policy Analysis and Management* 2 (Spring 1983):

350-65; Ralph Kramer, *Voluntary Agencies in the Welfare State* (Berkley: University of California Press, 1981); Lester M. Salamon and Alan J. Abramson, "The Nonprofit Sector," in Palmer and Sawhill, *The Reagan Experiment*; Burton A. Weisbrod, *The Voluntary Nonprofit Sector: An Economic Analysis* (Lexington, MA: Lexington, 1977).

42. The exceptions are: Nelson, "Purchase of Services"; and Wedel, et al, *Social Services*.

43. Noteworthy exceptions are: Phillip J. Cooper, "Government Contracts in Public Administration: The Role and Environment of the Contracting Offices," *Public Administration Review* 40 (Sept./Oct. 1980): 459-468; Martha Derthick, *Uncontrollable Spending for Social Service Grants* (Washington, DC: Brookings, 1975).

44. Ayres, "Municipal Interfaces"; Fitch, "Increasing the Role"; Hanrahan, *Government for $ale*.

45. "Increasing the Role," p. 279.

46. Neil Gilbert "The Transformation"; Eleanor Brilliant, "Private or Public: A Model of Ambiguities," *Social Service Review* 47 (September 1973): 384-96; Gordon Manser, "Implications of Purchase of Services for Voluntary Agencies," *Social Casework* 55 (July 1974): 421-7; Norman V. Lourie, "Purchase of Service Contracting: Issues Confronting the Government Sponsored Agency," Wedel, et al., *Social Services*, 18-29.

47. "The Transformation of Social Services," 633-4.

48. See, for example, Ira Sharkansky, "Policy Making and Service Delivery on the Margins of Government: The Case of Contractors," *Public Administration Review* 40 (March/April 1980): 116-123; Smith, *The New Political Economy*; Smith and D. C. Hague, eds., *The Dilemma of Accountability in Modern Government: Independence vs. Control* (New York: St. Martin's Press, 1971).

49. Brilliant, "Private or Public," in particular, makes this point.

50. Brilliant, "Private or Public"; Bertram Beck, "Governmental Contracts With the Non-Profit Social Welfare Corporations," in Smith and Hague, eds., *The Dilemma of Accountability*.

51. Kettl, "The Fourth Face."

52. "Benton Harbor City Manager Proposes Laying Off Most Employees," *The Benton Harbor Herald-Palladium*, (Feb. 3, 1981): A1.

53. See Hanrahan, *Government for $ale*.

54. "Private or Public," 394.

55. *Bureaucracy*, 215.

56. "More Bang."

57. Bennett and Johnson, *Better Government*.

Chapter Two

1. Other scholars might select a slightly different number or set of conditions from the literature, but I believe these three are the most obvious and significant features necessary for contracting out to work as envisioned by proponents.

2. Admittedly, the goal of cost reduction does not necessarily require a maximizing assumption. Conceivably, the expected outcomes could often be realized with satisficing behavior by officials, in the Herbert Simon tradition. But most of the theoretical contracting literature implies a maximizing principle. See James March and Simon, *Organizations* (New York: Wiley and Sons, 1958); Vincent Ostrom, *The Intellectual Crisis in American Public Administration*, rev. ed. (University, AL: University of Alabama Press, 1974), 50-52.

3. These connections have been made in some of the more applied works in public administration and human services. See, for example, Barbara J. Nelson, "Purchase of Services," in George Washnis, ed., *Productivity Improvement Handbook for State and Local Governments* (Washington, DC: National Academy of Public Administration, 1980), 427-447; and Kenneth R. Wedel, Arthur J. Katz, and Ann Weick, eds., *Social Services By Government Contract: A Policy Analysis* (New York: Praeger, 1979).

4. In doing this, I am undoubtedly simplifying complex arguments, placing together scholars who would not see themselves as members of a common 'school,' and making generalizations that may not accurately represent any single scholar's contribution. This is an inevitable consequence of any enterprise that attempts to synthesize a complex, diverse literature.

5. Pioneering works in this tradition are Arthur R. Burns, *The Decline of Competition* (New York: McGraw-Hill, 1936); Edward Chamberlin, *The Theory of Monopolistic Competition* (Cambridge, MA: Harvard University Press, 1933); Joan Robinson, *The Economics of Imperfect Competition* (London: Macmillan, 1933); John Von Neumann and Oskar Morgenstern, *The Theory of Games and Economic Behavior* (Princeton, NJ: Princeton University Press, 1947). Themes developed in these early works have been elaborated on by various economists in the liberal tradition. See, for example, Joe S. Bain, *Barriers to New Competition* (Cambridge, MA: Harvard University Press, 1956); W. G. Shepherd, *Market Power and Economic Welfare* (New York: Random House, 1970); Martin Shubik, *Strategy and Market Structure* (New York: Wiley, 1959). For an

extension of economic concepts to government activity, see, for example, Randall Bartlett, *Economic Foundations of Political Power* (New York: The Free Press, 1973) esp. ch. 1-7, 12-15.

6. The best examples of pluralist thought include Robert A. Dahl, *Who Governs?* (New Haven, CT: Yale University Press, 1961); Nelson W. Polsby, *Community Power and Political Theory* (New Haven, CT: Yale University Press, 1963); David B. Truman, *The Governmental Process* (New York: Alfred A. Knopf, 1951).

7. The major works in this tradition are E. E. Schattschneider, *The Semi-Sovereign People* (New York: Holt, Rinehart and Winston, 1960); Henry S. Kariel, *The Decline of American Pluralism* (Palo Alto, CA: Stanford University Press, 1961); Grant McConnell, *Private Power and American Democracy* (New York: Knopf, 1966); William E. Connolly, ed., *The Bias of Pluralism* (New York: Atherton, 1969); Theodore Lowi, *The End of Liberalism* (New York: W. W. Norton, 1969). The original term and phenomenon of cooptation was explained in a classic sociological work, Philip Selznick, *TVA and the Grass Roots* (Berkley: University of California Press, 1949). These works can also be classified as part of a larger body of literature that emphasizes clientelism—the power relationship between government agencies and major constituent/client interests. See, for example, Norton E. Long, "Power and Administration," *Public Administration Review* 9 (Autumn 1949): 257-264; Francis E. Rourke, *Bureaucracy, Politics, and Public Policy* (Boston: Little, Brown, 1969); and Herbert Simon, Donald W. Smithburg, and Victor A. Thompson, *Public Administration* (New York: Knopf, 1950). More recently, works in the regulatory and general public policy literature have focused on the phenomena of issue networks, iron triangles, agency capture, and subsystem politics.

8. Bruce L. R. Smith, "Accountability and Independence in the Contract State," Smith and D. C. Hague, eds., *The Dilemma of Accountability in Modern Government* (New York: St. Martin's, 1971).

9. Metzenbaum, NBC Television Interview, *Today*, May 21, 1981.

10. Gordon Adams, *The Iron Triangle: The Politics of Defense Contracting* (New York: Council on Economic Priorities, 1981).

11. Gordon Tullock, *The Politics of Bureaucracy* (Washington, D.C.: Public Affairs Press, 1965); William A. Niskanen, Jr., *Bureaucracy and Representative Government* (Chicago: Aldine-Atherton, 1971).

12. On the other hand, contracting opponents seem to blame most corruption and opportunism on the contractors and downplay the issue of gains by officials.

13. These classic decision-making works include Herbert Simon, *Administrative Behavior* (New York: Macmillan, 1947); Simon, *Models of*

Man (New York: John Wiley and Sons, 1957); James G. March and Simon, *Organizations*; Richard M. Cyert and March, *A Behavioral Theory of the Firm* (Englewood Cliffs, NJ: Prentice-Hall, 1963); Charles E. Lindblom, "The Science of 'Muddling Through' " *Public Administration Review* 19 (Spring, 1959): 79-88; Lindblom and David Braybrooke, *A Strategy of Decision* (New York: Free Press of Glencoe, 1963); Anthony Downs, *Inside Bureaucracy* (Boston: Little, Brown, 1966). This perspective draws in part from Graham T. Allison's second model, labelled an Organizational Process Model. See especially Allison's third chapter, *Essence of Decision: Explaining the Cuban Missile Crisis* (Boston: Little, Brown, 1971).

Chapter Three

1. See the following for explanations of the legislation and summaries and comparisons of the states' activities in these areas: Bill Benton, Tracey Feild, and Rhona Millar, *Social Services: Federal Legislation vs. State Implementation* (Washington, DC: Urban Institute, 1978); National Governors' Association, *Utilization of Governors' Discretionary Grant Funds Under CETA* (Washington, DC: National Governors' Association, 1978); Peter S. O'Donnell, *Social Services: Three Years After Title XX* (Washington, DC: National Governors' Association, 1978). For an overview of welfare and employment programs and their backgrounds, see, for example, Andrew W. Dobelstein, *Politics, Economics, and Public Welfare* (Englewood Cliffs, NJ: Prentice-Hall, 1980); and Sar A. Levitan, *Programs in Aid of the Poor for the 1980s*, 4th ed. (Baltimore, MD: Johns Hopkins University Press, 1980).

2. Michigan House Fiscal Agency, *Purchasing Social Services Under Title XX in Michigan* (Lansing, MI: Michigan House of Representatives, 1976).

3. Title XX Administration Division, Department of Social Services, *Michigan Annual Title XX Services Plan 1979-1980* (Lansing, MI, 1979).

4. Michigan Department of Labor, Bureau of Employment and Training, *Annual Plan for Special Grants to Governors, Comprehensive Employment and Training Act* (Lansing, MI, 1980).

5. Jeffrey D. Straussman and John Farie, "Contracting for Social Services at the Local Level," *Urban Interest* 3 (Spring, 1981): 43.

6. Michigan House Fiscal Agency, *Purchasing Social Services*.

7. Since this research, Title XX has been changed and renamed the

Social Service Block Grant, under the Omnibus Budget Reconciliation Act of 1981. One of the changed provisions included the elimination of the state matching requirement. For an overview of the Reagan administration's approach to the policy area of social services, see Michael F. Gutowski and Jeffrey J. Koshel, "Social Services," in John L. Palmer and Isabel V. Sawhill, eds., *The Reagan Experiment* (Washington, DC: Urban Institute, 1982), 307-28. For the likely effects of Reagan's Economic Recovery Program on nonprofit agencies, see Lester M. Salamon and Alan J. Abramson, "The Nonprofit Sector," in Palmer and Sawhill, 219-43.

8. *Politics, Economics, and Public Welfare*, 222.

9. For the development of social services legislation under Title XX, see Paul E. Mott, *Meeting Human Needs: The Social and Political History of Title XX* (Columbus, OH: National Conference on Social Service, 1976).

10. For the interesting political-administrative background of the legislation and the effect on HEW, see Martha Derthick, *Uncontrollable Spending for Social Services* (Washington, DC: Brookings, 1975), especially chapter 10.

11. Michigan House Fiscal Agency, *Purchasing Social Services*, 4.

12. *Purchasing Social Services*, 38.

13. Derthick, *Uncontrollable Spending*, chapters 3-8. Some of the other states, however, were more involved in purchasing existing services from other state agencies.

14. Benton, Feild, and Millar, *Social Services*, 50-1.

15. National Governors' Association, *Utilization of Governors' Discretionary Grant Funds*.

16. As it was, one of the agencies originally selected for an interview had disbanded after the end of its Title IV contract. Another agency was chosen to be interviewed in its place.

17. These did not include the several research contracts with private agencies.

18. Obviously, the agency that was mentioned in note sixteen did not fare so well without the funds.

Chapter Four

1. The Council of State Government, *State and Local Government Purchasing* (Lexington, KY: COS, 1975), especially chapter 6.

2. If officials believed that the unsolicited proposal contained a needed service and a good service delivery plan, they either: 1) awarded a contract without trying to compare the proposal to any others, when there were unexpended funds; or 2) requested that the agency resubmit the proposal at the annual proposal evaluation time in the contracting cycle to consider it along with other proposals. The limits on federal funds have meant that in the last few years few of these proposals have led to awards.

3. Usually written by the contract coordinator with assistance from program staff, this information gave the requirements for the contract and outlined the proposal format. The requirements usually included the following: acceptable total cost range, equal opportunity employment, affirmative action program, length of the contract (usually one year), the approximate number and type of clients to be served, the twenty-five percent donation regulations, record-keeping practices, and general types of services desired.

Chapter Five

1. Jacque E. Gibbons, "Needs Assessment in Purchase of Service Contracting," Kenneth R. Wedel, Arthur J. Katz, and Ann Weick, eds., *Social Services by Government Contract: A Policy Analysis* (New York: Praeger, 1979), 72.

2. See especially Gibbons, "Needs Assessment," and Bill Benton, Tracey Feild, and Rhona Millar, *Social Services: Federal Legislation vs. State Implementation* (Washington, DC: Urban Institute, 1978), especially chapter 2.

3. Memorandum from Fred Lawless, Director of Field Services Administration, to local office managers (March 27, 1979), Attachment A.

4. Memorandum from Fred Lawless, to local office managers (April 18, 1979).

5. It is possible, however, that although the general pattern is not cooptative, some coordinators may have occasionally preferred certain agencies because of friendships.

6. To clarify the question, I added the phrase, "instead of, for example, an expanded BET or MESC" (Michigan Employment Security Commission—a part of DOL, with branch offices throughout the state). This example seemed necessary after the pretest indicated that respondents needed an example to understand the question. It was clear that most respondents had never considered this question before.

7. Benton, Feild, and Millar, *Social Services*.

Chapter Seven

1. Two providers mentioned a report that documents this for counseling services and argues for increased utilization of private agencies: Michigan Federation of Child and Family Agencies, *In Partnership with the Public* (Lansing, MI: 1979), 15-18.
2. Martha Derthick, *Uncontrollable Spending for Social Services Grants* (Washington, DC: Brookings, 1975), 100.
3. Bill Benton, Tracey Feild and Rhona Millar, *Social Services: Federal Legislation vs. State Implementation* (Washington, DC: Urban Institute, 1978), 111.
4. I asked this question only because a couple of the officials in the early, unstructured interviews used the term 'democratic' to describe a perceived advantage of contracting out. To explore more fully what was meant by this, I included the probe 'Why?' if respondents said they saw a connection.
5. See, for example, Robert M. Spann, "Public versus Private Provision of Governmental Services," Thomas E. Borcherding, ed., *Budgets and Bureaucrats: The Sources of Government Growth* (Durham, NC: Duke University Press, 1977), 71-89.

Chapter Eight

1. Jeffrey D. Straussman and John Farie, "Contracting for Social Services at the Local Level," *The Urban Interest* 3 (Spring 1981): 43-50.
2. Kenneth R. Wedel, Arthur J. Katz, and Ann Weick, eds., *Social Services by Government Contract: A Policy Analysis* (New York: Praeger, 1979).
3. Phillip J. Cooper, "Government Contracting in Public Administration: The Role and Environment of the Contracting Officer," *Public Administration Review* 50 (Sept./Oct. 1980): 459.
4. Richard R. Nelson, *The Moon and the Ghetto* (New York: W. W. Norton, 1977), 47-50.
5. Walter Williams, *The Implementation Perspective: A Guide for Managing Social Service Delivery Systems* (Berkley, CA: University of California Press, 1980), 79.
6. Williams, *The Implementation Perspective*, 80.
7. Bruce L. R. Smith and D. C. Hague, eds., *The Dilemma of Accountability in Modern Government: Independence vs. Control* (New York: St. Martin's 1971).

References

Adams, Gordon. *The Iron Triangle: The Politics of Defense Contracting.* New York: Council on Economic Priorities, 1981.

Ahlbrandt, Roger S., Jr. "Efficiency in the Provision of Fire Services." *Public Choice* 18 (Fall 1973): 1-15.

Allison, Graham T. *Essence of Decision: Explaining the Cuban Missile Crisis.* Boston: Little, Brown, 1971.

The Antitrust Committee, National Association of Attorneys General, and The Committee on Competition in Governmental Purchasing, National Association of State Purchasing Officials. *Impediments to Competitive Bidding: How to Detect and Combat Them.* The Council of State Governments, 1963.

Ayres, Douglas W. "Municipal Interfaces in the Third Sector: A Negative View." *Public Administration Review* 35 (Sept./Oct. 1975) 459-63.

Bain, Joe S. *Barriers to New Competition.* Cambridge, MA: Harvard University Press, 1956.

Baker, Keith G. "Public-Choice Theory: Some Important Assumptions and Public-Policy Implications." Robert T. Golembiewski, et al. *Public Administration: Readings in Institutions, Processes, Behavior, Policy,* 3rd ed. Chicago: Rand McNally, 1976, 41-60.

Bartlett, Randall. *Economic Foundations of Political Power.* New York: The Free Press, 1973.

Beck, Bertram. "Governmental Contracts with Non-Profit Social Welfare Corporations," Bruce L. R. Smith and D. C. Hague, eds. *The Dilemma of Accountability in Modern Government: Independence Versus Control.* New York: St. Martin's, 1971, 213-229.

Bennett, James T., and Manuel H. Johnson. *Better Government at Half the Price.* Ottawa, IL: Caroline House, 1981.

———. "Public versus Private Provision of Collective Goods and Services: Garbage Collection Revisited." *Public Choice* 34 (1979): 55-64.

———. "Tax Reduction Without Sacrifice: Private Sector Production of Public Service." *Public Finance Quarterly* 8 (Oct. 1980): 363-96.

Benton, Bill, Tracey Feild, and Rhona Millar. *Social Services: Federal Legislation vs. State Implementation.* Washington, DC: The Urban Institute, 1978.
Berger, Peter L., and Richard John Neuhaus. *To Empower People.* Washington, DC: American Enterprise Institute, 1977.
Bish, Robert L. *The Public Economy of Metropolitan Areas.* Chicago: Markham, 1971.
Bish, Robert L., and Vincent Ostrom. *Understanding Urban Government: Metropolitan Reform Reconsidered.* Washington, DC: American Enterprise Institute, 1973.
Borcherding, Thomas E., ed. *Budgets and Bureaucrats: The Sources of Government Growth.* Durham, NC: Duke University Press, 1977.
Brilliant, Eleanor. "Private or Public: A Model of Ambiguities." *Social Service Review* 47 (Sept. 1973): 384-396.
Buchanen, James M. "Why Does Government Grow?" Thomas E. Borcherding, ed. *Budgets and Bureaucrats: The Sources of Government Growth.* Durham, NC: Duke University Press, 1977, 3-18.
Burns, Arthur R. *The Decline of Competition.* New York: McGraw-Hill, 1936.
Chamberlin, Edward. *The Theory of Monopolistic Competition.* Cambridge, MA: Harvard University Press, 1933.
Cooper, Phillip J. "Government Contracts in Public Administration: The Role and Environment of the Contracting Officer." *Public Administration Review* 50 (Sept./Oct., 1980): 459-468.
The Council of State Governments. *State and Local Government Purchasing.* Lexington, KY: Council of State Governments, 1975.
Crozier, Michel. *The Bureaucratic Phenomenon.* Chicago: The University of Chicago Press, 1964.
Cyert, Richard M., and James G. March. *A Behavioral Theory of the Firm.* Englewood Cliffs, NJ: Prentice-Hall, 1963.
Dahl, Robert A. *Who Governs? Democracy and Power in an American City.* New Haven, CT: Yale University Press, 1961.
Danhof, Clarence. *Government Contracting and Technological Change.* Washington, DC: The Brookings Institution, 1968.
Davies, David G. "The Efficiency of Public versus Private Firms: The Case of Australia's Two Airlines." *Journal of Law and Economics* 14 (April, 1971): 149-65.
Deacon, Robert T. "The Expenditure Effects of Alternative Public Supply Institutions." *Public Choice* 34 (1979): 381-397.
De Alessi, Louis. "An Economic Analysis of Government Ownership and

Regulation: Theory and the Evidence From the Electric Power Industry." *Public Choice* 19 (Fall 1974): 1-42.
Derthick, Martha. *Uncontrollable Spending for Social Service Grants.* Washington, DC: Brookings Institution, 1975.
Dexter, Lewis Anthony. *Elite and Specialized Interviewing.* Evanston, IL: Northwestern University Press, 1970.
Dobelstein, Andrew W. *Politics, Economics, and Public Welfare.* Englewood Cliffs, NJ: Prentice-Hall, 1980.
Downs, Anthony. *Inside Bureaucracy.* Boston: Little, Brown, 1966.
Drucker, Peter F. *The Age of Discontinuity: Guidelines to Our Changing Society.* New York: Harper and Row, 1969.
———. "The Sickness of Government." *Public Interest* 14 (Winter 1969: 3-23.
Fesler, James W. *Public Administration: Theory and Practice.* Englewood Cliffs, NJ: Prentice-Hall, 1980, 292-302.
Fisk, Donald, Herbert Kiesling and Thomas Muller. *Private Provision of of Public Services: An Overview.* Washington, DC: The Urban Institute, 1978.
Fitch, Lyle C. "Increasing the Role of the Private Sector in Providing Public Services." Willis D. Hawley and David Rogers, eds. *Improving the Quality of Urban Management.* Beverly Hills, CA: Sage Publications, 1974, 264-306.
Florestano, Patricia S., and Stephen B. Gordon. "Public vs. Private: Small Government Contracting With the Private Sector." *Public Administration Review* 40 (Jan./Feb. 1980): 29-34.
Frankfather, Dwight L. "Welfare Entrepreneurialism and the Politics of Innovation." *Social Services Review* 55 (March 1981): 129-146.
Friedman, Milton. *Capitalism and Freedom.* Chicago: University of Chicago Press, 1962.
Garson, G. David. *Group Theories of Politics.* Beverly Hills, CA: Sage, 1978.
Gibbons, Jacque E. "Needs Assessment in Purchase of Service Contracting." Kenneth R. Wedel, Arthur J. Katz, and Ann Weick, eds. *Social Services by Government Contract: A Policy Analysis.* New York: Praeger, 1979.
Gilbert, Neil. "The Transformation of Social Services." *Social Service Review* 51 (Dec. 1977): 624-641.
Gorden, Raymond L. *Interviewing: Strategy, Techniques, and Tactics.* Homewood, IL: Dorsey Press, 1969.
Gutowski, Michael F., and Jeffrey J. Koshel. "Social Services." John L.

Palmer and Isabel V. Sawhill, eds. *The Reagan Experiment.* Washington, DC: The Urban Institute Press, 1982, 307-328.

Hanrahan, John. *Government for $ale: Contracting-out—The New Patronage.* (Washington, DC: American Federation of State, County and Municipal Employees, 1977).

Hirsch, Werner Z. "Cost Functions of Government Service: Refuse Collection." *Review of Economics and Statistics* 47 (Feb. 1965): 85-93.

Hirschman, Albert O. *Exit, Voice and Loyalty.* Cambridge, MA: Harvard University Press, 1970.

Hyman, Herbert H. *Interviewing in Social Research.* Chicago: The University of Chicago Press, 1954, 1975.

James, Estelle. "How Nonprofits Grow: a Model." *Journal of Policy Analysis and Management* 2 (Spring 1983): 350-365.

Kariel, Henry S. *The Decline of American Pluralism.* Stanford: Stanford University Press, 1961.

Keehn, Norman H. "A World of Becoming: From Pluralism to Corporatism." *Polity* 9 (Fall, 1976): 19-39.

Kelso, William A. *American Democratic Theory: Pluralism and Its Critics.* Westpost, CT: Greenwood Press, 1978.

Kemper, Peter, and John M. Quigley. *The Economics of Refuse Collection.* Cambridge, MA: Ballinger, 1976.

Kettl, Donald F. "The Fourth Face of Federalism." *Public Administration Review* 41 (May/June 1981): 366-373.

Kramer, Ralph. "Voluntary Agencies and the Use of Public Funds: Some Policy Issues." *Social Service Review* 40 (Nov. 1966): 15-26.

———. *Voluntary Agencies in the Welfare State.* Berkeley: University of California Press, 1981.

Levenson, Rosaline. "Contractual Services in Government: Selected Bibliography on Practices in Federal, State, and Local Agencies, Education, and Foreign Countries." Council of Planning Librarians, *Exchange Bibliography* No. 980 (Feb. 1976): 1-58.

Levitan, Sar A. *Programs in Aid of the Poor for the 1980s.* 4th ed. Baltimore: Johns Hopkins University Press, 1980.

Lindblom, Charles E. *Politics and Markets.* New York: Basic Books, 1977.

———. "The Science of 'Muddling Through'." *Public Administration Review* 19 (Spring 1959): 79-88.

———. "Still Muddling, Not Yet Through." *Public Administration Review* 39 (Nov./Dec. 1979): 517-526.

———, and David Braybrooke. *A Strategy of Decision.* New York: Free Press of Glencoe, 1963.

Long, Norton E. "Power and Administration." *Public Administration Review* 9 (Autumn 1949): 257-264.

REFERENCES

Lourie, Norman V. "Purchase of Service Contracting: Issues Confronting the Government Sponsored Agency." Kenneth R. Wedel, Arthur J. Katz, and Ann Weick, eds. *Social Services by Government Contract: A Policy Analysis.* New York: Praeger, 1979, 18-29.

Lowery, David. "The Political Incentives of Government Contracting." *Social Science Quarterly* 63 (Sept. 1982): 517-29.

Lowi, Theodore J. *The End of Liberalism.* New York: Norton, 1969.

Manser, Gordon. "Implications of Purchase-of-Service for Voluntary Agencies." *Social Casework* 55 (July 1974): 421-27.

March, James, and Herbert Simon. *Organizations.* New York: John Wiley and Sons, 1958.

McConnell, Grant. *Private Power and American Democracy.* New York: Knopf, 1966.

Michigan Department of Labor, Bureau of Employment and Training. *Annual Plan for Special Grants to Governors Comprehensive Employment and Training Act, Fiscal Year 1981.* Lansing, MI: Michigan Department of Labor, 1980.

Michigan Department of Social Services, Title XX Administration Division. *Michigan Annual Title XX Services Plan 1970-1980.* Lansing, MI: Department of Social Services, 1979.

Michigan Federation of Child and Family Agencies, *In Partnership with the Public* Lansing, MI: 1979.

Michigan House Fiscal Agency. *Purchasing Social Services Under Title XX in Michigan.* Lansing, MI: Michigan House of Representatives, 1976.

Miller, Gary J. *Cities By Contract: The Politics of Municipal Incorporation.* Cambridge, MA: MIT Press, 1981.

Mueller, Dennis C. *Public Choice.* Cambridge, UK: Cambridge University Press, 1979.

Mott, Paul E. *Meeting Human Needs: The Social and Political History of Title XX.* Columbus, OH: National Conference on Social Welfare, 1976.

Murnane, Richard J. "How Clients' Characterists Affect Organization Performance." *Journal of Policy Analysis and Management* 2 (Spring 1983): 403-417.

National Governors' Association. *Utilization of Governors' Discretionary Grant Funds Under CETA.* Washington, DC: National Governors' Association, 1978.

Nelson, Barbara J. "Purchase of Services." George Washnis, ed. *Productivity Improvement Handbook for State and Local Governments.* Washington, DC: National Academy of Public Administration, 1980, 427-447.

Nelson, Richard R. *The Moon and the Ghetto.* New York: W. W. Norton & Co., 1977.

———, and Michael Krashinsky. "Public Control and Economic Organization of Day Care for Young Children." *Public Policy* (Winter, 1974): 53-75.

Niskanen, William A., Jr. *Bureaucracy and Representative Government.* Chicago: Aldine-Atherton, 1971.

O'Donnell, Peter S. *Social Services: Three Years After Title XX.* Washington, DC: National Governors' Association, 1978.

Olson, Mancur, Jr. *The Logic of Collective Action: Public Goods and the Theory of Groups.* Revised Ed. New York: Schocken Books, 1971.

Ostrom, Vincent. *The Intellectual Crisis in American Public Administration.* Revised Ed. University, AL: The University of Alabama Press, 1974.

———, and Elinor Ostrom. "Public Choice: A Different Approach to the Study of Public Administration." *Public Administration Review* 31 (March/April 1971): 203-216.

———. "Public Goods and Public Choices." E. S. Savas, ed. *Alternatives for Delivering Public Services Toward Improved Performance.* Boulder, CO: Westview Press, 1977, 7-49.

Palmer, John L. and Isabel V. Sawhill, eds. *The Reagan Experiment* Washington, DC: Urban Institute, 1982.

Payne, Stanley L. *The Art of Asking Questions.* Princeton, NJ: Princeton University Press, 1951.

Perrow, Charles. *Complex Organizations: A Critical Essay.* Glenview, IL: Scott, Foresman & Co., 1972.

Polsby, Nelson W. *Community Power and Political Theory.* New Haven, CT: Yale University Press, 1963.

Poole, Robert W., Jr. *Cutting Back City Hall.* New York: Universe Books, 1980.

Reagan, Michael D. *The Managed Economy.* London: Oxford University Press, 1963.

Robinson, Joan. *The Economics of Imperfect Competition.* London: Macmillan, 1933.

Rourke, Francis E. *Bureaucracy, Politics, and Public Policy.* Boston: Little, Brown, 1969.

Salamon, Lester M., and Alan J. Abramson. "The Nonprofit Sector." John L. Palmer and Isabel V. Sawhill, eds., *The Reagan Experiment.* Washington, DC: The Urban Institute Press, 1982, 219-243.

Samuelson, Paul. "The Pure Theory of Public Expenditure." *Review of Economics and Statistics* 36 (1954): 387-389.

Schultze, Charles L. *The Public Use of Private Interest.* Washington, DC: Brookings Institution, 1977.
Savas, E. S., ed. *Alternatives for Delivering Public Services Toward Improved Performance.* Boulder, CO: Westview, 1977.
———·"An Empirical Study of Competition in Municipal Service Delivery." *Public Administration Review* 37 (Nov./Dec. 1977): 717-724.
———· "Intracity Competition Between Public and Private Service Delivery. *Public Administration Review* 41 (Jan./Feb. 1981): 46-52.
———· "Municipal Monopolies Versus Competition in Delivering Urban Services." Willis D. Hawley and David Rogers, eds. *Improving the Quality of Urban Management.* Beverly Hills, CA: Sage, 1974, 473-500.
———· *The Organization and Efficiency of Solid Waste Collection.* Lexington, MA: Lexington Books, 1977.
———· "Policy Analysis for Local Government: Public vs. Private Refuse Collection." *Policy Analysis* 3 (Winter 1977): 49-74.
———· "Public vs. Private Refuse Collection: A Critical Review of the Evidence." *Journal of Urban Analysis* 6 (July 1979): 1-13.
———· "Solid Waste Collection in Metropolitan Areas." Elinor Ostrom, ed. *The Delivery of Urban Services,* Vol. 10 of *Urban Affairs Annual Reviews* (Beverly Hills, CA: Sage, 1976): 201-29.
———, Barbara J. Stevens, and Eileen B. Berenyi. "Solid Waste Collection: Organization and Efficiency of Service Delivery," Judith V. May and Aaron B. Wildavsky, eds. *The Policy Cycle.* Beverly Hills, CA: Sage, 1978, 145-165.
Schattsneider, E. E. *The Semi-Sovereign People.* New York: Holt, Rinehart and Winston, 1960.
Seidman, Harold. *Politics, Position and Power.* New York: Oxford University Press, 1970.
Selznick, Philip. *TVA and the Grass Roots.* Berkeley: University of California Press, 1949.
Sharkansky, Ira. "Policy Making and Service Delivery on the Margins of Government: The Case of Contractors." *Public Administration Review* 40 (March/April 1980): 116-123.
———· *Wither the State? Politics and Public Enterprise in Three Countries.* Chatham, NJ: Chatham House, 1979.
Shepherd, W. G. *Market Power and Economic Welfare.* New York: Random House, 1970.
Sherman, Stanley N. *Procurement Management: The Federal System.* Bethesda, MD: SL Communications, 1979.

Shubik, Martin. *Strategy and Market Structure.* New York: Wiley, 1959.
Simon, Herbert. *Models of Man.* New York: John Wiley and Sons, 1957.
―――. *Administrative Behavior.* Second Edition. New York: Macmillan, 1961.
―――. Donald W. Smithburg, and Victor A. Thompson. *Public Administration.* New York: Knopf, 1950.
Smith, Bruce L. R. *The New Political Economy.* New York: St. Martin's, 1975.
―――, and D. C. Hague, eds. *The Dilemma of Accountability in Modern Government: Independence vs. Control.* New York: St. Martin's, 1971.
Sonenblum, Sidney, John J. Kirlin, and John C. Ries. *How Cities Provide Services: An Evaluation of Alternative Delivery Structures.* Cambridge, MA: Ballinger, 1977.
Spann, Robert M. "Collective Consumption of Private Goods." *Public Choice* 20 (Winter 1974): 63-81.
―――. "Public Versus Private Provision of Governmental Services." Thomas E. Borcherding, ed. *Budgets and Bureaucrats: The Sources of Government Growth.* Durham, NC: Duke University Press, 1977, 71-89.
Straussman, Jeffrey D. "More Bang for Fewer Bucks? Or How Local Governments Can Rediscover the Potentials (and Pitfalls) of the Market." *Public Administration Review* 41 (Special Issue, 1981): 150-7.
―――, and John Farie. "Contracting for Social Services at the Local Level." *Urban Interest* 3 (Spring, 1981): 43-50.
Terrell, Paul. "Private Alternatives to Public Human Services Administration." *Social Service Review* 53 (March 1979): 56-74.
Thompson, Victor. *Modern Organization.* New York: Alfred A. Knopf, 1961.
Truman, David B. *The Governmental Process.* New York: Alfred A. Knopf, 1951.
Tullock, Gordon. *The Politics of Bureaucracy.* Washington, DC: Public Affairs Press, 1965.
U.S. Department of Labor. Employment and Training Administration. CETA Rules and Regulations. *Federal Register.* (May 20, 1980): Part IX Vol. 45, 33843-33923.
Von Neumann, John, and Oskar Morgenstern. *The Theory of Games and Economic Behavior.* Princeton, NJ: Princeton University Press, 1947.

Wamsley, Gary L., and Mayer N. Zald. *The Political Economy of Public Organizations: A Critique and Approach to the Study of Public Administration.* Bloomington, IN: Indiana University Press, 1976.

Warren, Robert O. *Government in Metropolitan Regions: A Reappraisal of Fractionated Political Organization.* Davis, CA: Institute of Governmental Affairs, 1966.

Warwick, Donald P. *A Theory of Public Bureaucracy: Politics, Personality, and Organization in the State Department.* Cambridge, MA: Harvard University Press, 1975.

Weber, Max. *From Max Weber: Essays in Sociology,* translated, edited, with introduction by H. H. Gerth and C. Wright Mills. New York: Oxford University Press, 1958.

Wedel, Kenneth R. "Government Contracting for Purchase of Service." *Social Work* 21 (March 1976): 101–5.

———, Arthur J. Katz, and Ann Weick, eds. *Social Services by Government Contract: A Policy Analysis.* New York: Praeger, 1979.

Weisbrod, Burton A. *The Voluntary Nonprofit Sector: An Economic Analysis.* Lexington, MA: Lexington Books, 1977.

Williams, Walter. *The Implementation Perspective.* Berkeley, CA: University of California Press, 1980.

Wolf, Charles, Jr. "A Theory of Non-Market Failures." *The Public Interest* 55 (Spring 1979): 114–33.

Woodward, Joan. *Industrial Organization: Theory and Practice.* London: Oxford University Press, 1965.

Young, Dennis R. "Institutional Change and the Delivery of Urban Public Services." *Policy Sciences* 2 (Dec. 1971): 425–438.

———, and Richard R. Nelson, eds. *Public Policy for Day Care of Young Children.* Lexington, MA: Lexington Books, 1973.

Index

Accountability, 13-14
Agreements (client/provider), 42
Award Process, 79

Bennett, James T., 9, 10
Bidding. *See* Government contracts
Brilliant, Eleanor, 15*n*
Buchanan, James M., 7*n*
Bureaucracy, criticism of, 1-2, 4
Bureaucrats (and contractors), 80-83, 93-95
Bureau of Employment and Training (BET, Michigan):
  case study, 46-52
  compared with DSS, 130-33
  and competition, 62-69
  and contract decision making, 71, 86-100
  costs and benefits of contracting out, 120-27
  review procedures, 107-12

Community based organizations (CBO's), 63-64, 93
Competition, 18-19, 22, 130
  in service environments, 54-70
Comprehensive Employment and Training Act (CETA), 36, 46-52
  and competition, 63-67
  and contract decision making, 86-98
Contract bidding. *See* Government contracts
Contract cities plan (California), 3, 8

Contracting out, 3, 32-33, 141-43
  advantages of, 4-7
  and competition, 54-70, 130
  conditions for success, 18-21
  and cooptation, 25-28, 39-40, 138
  costs and benefits of, 113-28
  disadvantages of, 12-16
  human services case studies, 34-53
  literature on, 7-12
  market imperfections, economics of, 22-24, 138
  organizational decision making, 28-31, 70-100, 131-33, 138-41
  realities of, 133-37
  review procedures, 101-12
Contractors, 23-24, 55-57
  and bureaucrats, 80-83, 93-95
  choosing, 76-79, 88-93
  and politicians, 83-86, 95-96
Cooper, Phillip J., 135*n*
Cooptation, 25-28, 39-40, 100, 138
Corruption (in government), 12-13
Costs and benefits (of contracting out), 79, 113-28
Cyert, Richard M., 29

Decision making process, 19-20, 25. *See also* Organizational decision making
Demand, 22-24
Department of Defense (DOD), 13, 23, 27
Department of Labor (DOL, Michigan), 36, 46-52, 65. *See also* Bureau of Employment and Training

INDEX

Department of Social Services (DSS, Michigan):
case study, 36–46
compared with BET, 130–33
and competition, 55–62, 67–69
and contract decision making, 70–86, 96–100
costs and benefits of contracting out, 114–20
review procedures, 102–107, 111–12
Derthick, Martha, 44n
Dobelstein, Andrew W., 43n
Donated funds, 42, 44, 57–59

Economic Recovery Program, 2
Empirical literature, review of, 7–12
Employment services, 46–52. *See also* Bureau of Employment and Training

Farie, John, 37, 133
Federal contracts. *See* Government contracts
Fitch, Lyle C., 12n

Gilbert, Neil, 13n
Government:
contracting out, history of, 3
corruption in, 12–13
criticism of, 1–2
decision making process, 19–20, 25
role in contracting out, 4–5
watchdog role, 20–21, 39, 101–12, 133
See also Contracting out
Government contracts:
bidding process, 18–19
and competition, 54–70
and cooptation, 26–28
Governors' Grants, 47–48, 51
Governors' Special State-Wide Youth Services, 48

Hague, D. C., 142
Hard services, 10–11
Health, Education and Welfare, Department of (HEW), 43
Hirschman, Albert O., 7
Housing and Urban Development, Department of (HUD), 2

Human services, 9, 10, 13, 14, 34–37. *See also* Employment services; Social services

Information, 22–24

Job Training Partnership Act (1982), 46
Johnson, Manuel H., 9, 10

Kettl, Donald F., 11

Labor unions, 14–15
Lakewood Plan (California), 3, 8
Lindbloom, Charles E., 29–30
Lowery, David, 10
Lowi, Theodore, 25, 26

McConnell, Grant, 25
Manpower Programs, 63
March, James G., 29
Market imperfection, economics of, 22–24, 138
Metzenbaum, Howard, 27
Michigan Employment Training Council (METC), 87, 89

Needs assessments:
in Bureau of Employment and Training, 87–88
in Department of Social Services, 74–76
Niskanen, William A., 4–5, 15, 28
Nonprofit sector, 11, 13

Office of Management and Budget (OMB), 2
On-the-job training (OJT), 88
Opportunities Industrialization Centers (OIC), 63
Organizational decision making, 19–20, 28–32, 70–100, 131–33, 138–41

Planning:
in Bureau of Employment and Training, 87–88
in Department of Social Services, 74–76
Pluralism, 25

Politicians (and contractors), 83-86, 95-96
Pork barreling, 73
Private sector, 2-3, 5, 8, 11, 13, 63-64
Proposal writing, 61-62, 66-69, 80, 88-93, 98
Public choice theorists, 4-5, 17-24, 135
Public employees, 14-15
Public policy, 14
Public sector, 63-64
Purchased social services, 42-43, 128
  in Bureau of Employment and Training, 120-26
  in Department of Social Services, 114-19
  problems with, 119-20, 126-27

Rational decision making, 28-30, 71, 131-33
Reagan, Ronald, 2
Request For Proposal (RFP), 61-62, 66-69, 88-93, 98
Review Process, 27-28
  in Bureau of Employment and Training, 107-12
  in Department of Social Services, 102-107, 111-12

Savas, E. S., 5, 9, 10
Simon, Herbert, 29
Smith, Bruce L. R., 3, 27, 142

Social Security Act (1975, rev.), 36
Social services, 38-46. *See also* Department of Social Services
Soft services, 10-11
Solicitation (of contracts), 61-62, 88-93
Straussman, Jeffrey D., 15-16, 37, 133
Suppliers, 23-24
Supply, 22-24
Supply side economics, 2, 4-5

Title XX (Social Security Act), 36-38, 40, 42-46
  and competition, 57-60
  and contract decision making, 71-77, 86-98
Titles II and IV (CETA), 36, 46-52, 64-67, 86-98
Training services. *See* Employment services
Tullock, Gordon, 28

Urban Institute, 44-45*n*, 97*n*

Vouchers, 5

Watchdog role of government, 20-21, 39, 101-12, 133
Wedel, Kenneth R., 134

Youth services contracts, 48, 88-92, 100